Systemic Co

The organisation as

Systemic Consulting – *The organisation as a living system*

Siebke Kaat and Anton de Kroon

Editing: James G. Campbell

Translation by: Anton de Kroon

Originally published under title: Systemisch adviseren

© 2017, Systemic Books Publishing

ISBN 978-1539788454 (NUR 801)

Contents

Preface

In this book Siebke Kaat and Anton de Kroon are walking a new path.

Systemic-phenomenological work originally began with the method called constellations (family and organisational), which is now known far and wide. During the last 15 years constellations have taught us how social systems, including organisations, are put together. The focus, naturally enough, fell upon the quite spectacular method of constellations; the disadvantage here is that the quality of the method depends very much on the person applying it, the facilitator of the constellation. Siebke and Anton have made a complete U turn, by focussing on making the systemic body of thought applicable without being dependent upon constellations. It provides you with a tremendous feeling of pleasure when, with the perfect question or observation, you suddenly feel light streaming into a problem again. Well, you don't master the art of true systemic perception in five minutes. However, what you can do in five minutes is begin to familiarise yourself with its language.

Siebke and Anton are professionals with broad and practical experience. They are clear people, firmly grounded – not afraid to get their hands dirty - but never just drifting along. Already, for over a decade, they have been using systemic perception in their practices as consultants and, even more importantly, in their everyday lives. Systemic intervention is actually more a deliberate and permanent approach than a temporary tool. You are it rather than do it. In the same way that a craftsman's chisel becomes a part of him. From the outside it looks as if it is only the hammer that hits the chisel; inside him a very different process is going on. This is the systemic way; the way of Siebke and Anton.

In this book you'll accompany them and, quite often, they'll let you go off on your own. Trusting you and certain that, with the systemic compass to hand, you will have a pleasant and helpful instrument to guide you through the forest that is called an organisation.

Jan Jacob Stam

Thank you

Here, in front of you, lies a book on systemic consulting. For us, the authors, it is more than that. It also represents our own development as we grew into becoming systemic consultants. The road we travelled is one without a clear starting point and most certainly without a clear point of arrival. Development carries on.

Thank you to everyone standing behind and beside us.

A great number of experiences, courses, teachers, colleagues, assignments and talks have formed both of us. They provided us with a leg-up when needed and moments of reflection that contributed significantly to our development. Even if we do not name them here, all have their place. We sincerely wish that each one of them recognises a little of their ideas or situations in this book.

In addition there are the people who stimulated us to share our development and our views about our profession in the form of a book.

Participants, in courses we gave, asking us to write down what we were saying, were a stimulus to do just that. Jan Jacob Stam certainly played that role as well; from his intense involvement with the systemic approach he is always inspiring experiments and innovation. At just the right moment he would ask *"How are you doing with the book?"*

Finally, this book would not have come into existence without support, during the writing process, from the people in our personal lives who gave us the time and space the work demanded and those who read the manuscripts and made valuable suggestions.

Thanks to all the organisations.

Our thanks to our clients, the organisations and their people, for whom we worked over a number of years, and where we were able to learn about this living organism called an 'organisation'.

Innovation and growth come to life via exchange. In trusting to let go of habitual approaches and concepts, the option of renewal is revealed. Through our work we learned new paths and new ways to walk them. All the examples in this book derive from our own practice; they are a small window into a much larger body of work.

How could we, the authors, possibly restore the balance in taking and giving with everyone who has contributed, over the years, to our development and, through that, to this book? The most precious gift is, possibly, that we have nurtured ourselves with what we received and have passed it on to others: organisations, consultants and managers.

With gratitude,

Anton de Kroon

Siebke Kaat

Introduction

Consultants are usually invited to work in an organisation when its own managers are unable to find solutions to business problems. Then expert help is brought in – on a temporary basis.

Systemic consulting is uniquely different from any other consulting approach in that it is not the consultant who is the expert, but the organisation itself. What then is there for the consultant to do? That is what this book is about.

How did it begin?

Systemic consulting is tremendously inspired by the body of thought that underlies working via organisational constellations. Once we learned to facilitate constellations, we started acting from that attitude and knowledge in our day-to-day consulting. Increasingly, we became successful in translating the guidelines for facilitating constellations into forms for our own attitude as consultants. And here, exactly as is the case with facilitating constellations, our awareness was, and is, a crucial source of information. By asking ordinary questions and making ordinary remarks we learned that, together with the client, team or internal consultant, we could gain insight into the way organisational systems react, move and survive.

Nature continues to amaze us. Looking at the exchange among all living creatures we are awestruck by the individual species and with the beautiful coherence between them all. By delving deeply into living systems, time and again the organisation appeared in our mind's eye as a specific kind of living system. Both a living system and also an ordinary system with needs, embedded in and dependent upon a bigger whole.

A wish

Via this book, we hope to encourage you to take a systemic view of organisations and to show you how you can contribute towards the vitality of the systems into which you are invited to help.

We are constantly walking two, if not three, paths in this book. Beside the theory we give plenty of examples from our own consultancy practices, in the hope that this makes the theory clearer for the reader and easier to apply in his or her own practice. We also suggest questions to help you begin your own systemic explorations.

Useful as our insights might be, it is important that we help you to find your own answers to the question *"That's all very fine but, as a consultant, what kind of interventions can I make, and what do I need to make them?"*

Examples we give are derived from our practice, which is not the same as the practice. For us they are connected to a specific time and space and, at the same time, they are general illustrations. Knowing who, where and when would destroy our message. Our wish is that you let yourself be taken by an all-embracing loving perspective, without any opinion or judgement about organisations and the people who, temporarily, populate them.

Structure of the book

We regard organisations as living systems. Our grasp of what makes a living system, its characteristics and to what degree one can recognise them in an organisation, is what we write about in the first chapter.

In chapter two we give an insight into the various sources of the systemic approach.

In the third chapter we look more deeply into organisations as living systems. We discuss the fundamental needs that must be fulfilled in order to create a perfectly-sound organisational system. We also describe some reaction patterns which organisations might show if one or more of these needs are not met.

In chapter four we encounter the systemic consultant. We start with the basic attitude needed to strengthen organisational systems and continue by elaborating what is so specific about the way the systemic consultant works.

There were two reasons for writing the short, fifth, chapter about systemic coaching. There is its relationship with systemic consulting and the fact that many consultants also work as coaches. As the focus of the book is on supporting and strengthening organisational systems, this chapter, about individual coaching, is quite short.

Consultants usually appear in organisations when something has gone wrong or when managers can't fix the problem themselves. But the systemic approach really can support the prevention of problems. It is satisfying when every person, carrying out their everyday tasks and duties, contributes easily to the vital energy of an organisation. As this is mainly in the hands of team leaders, managers and directors, chapter six offers some preventive and everyday systemic interventions as tools for these groups.

In the seventh and last chapter we will give you an idea of how to look systemically at the world around you.

Finally

We believe in growth by exchange. This book is a snapshot in time. There is so much more to know about this fascinating, living system called an organisation; we would love to continue our learning by walking the path of systemic-phenomenological work together with you.

So, we invite you to share your insights and experiences with us and with others.

Siebke Kaat and Anton de Kroon
January 2013

Siebke Kaat: siebke.kaat@pragmavision.nl
Anton de Kroon: ak@hellingerinstituut.nl
Linked-in group: systemische kijk op organisaties

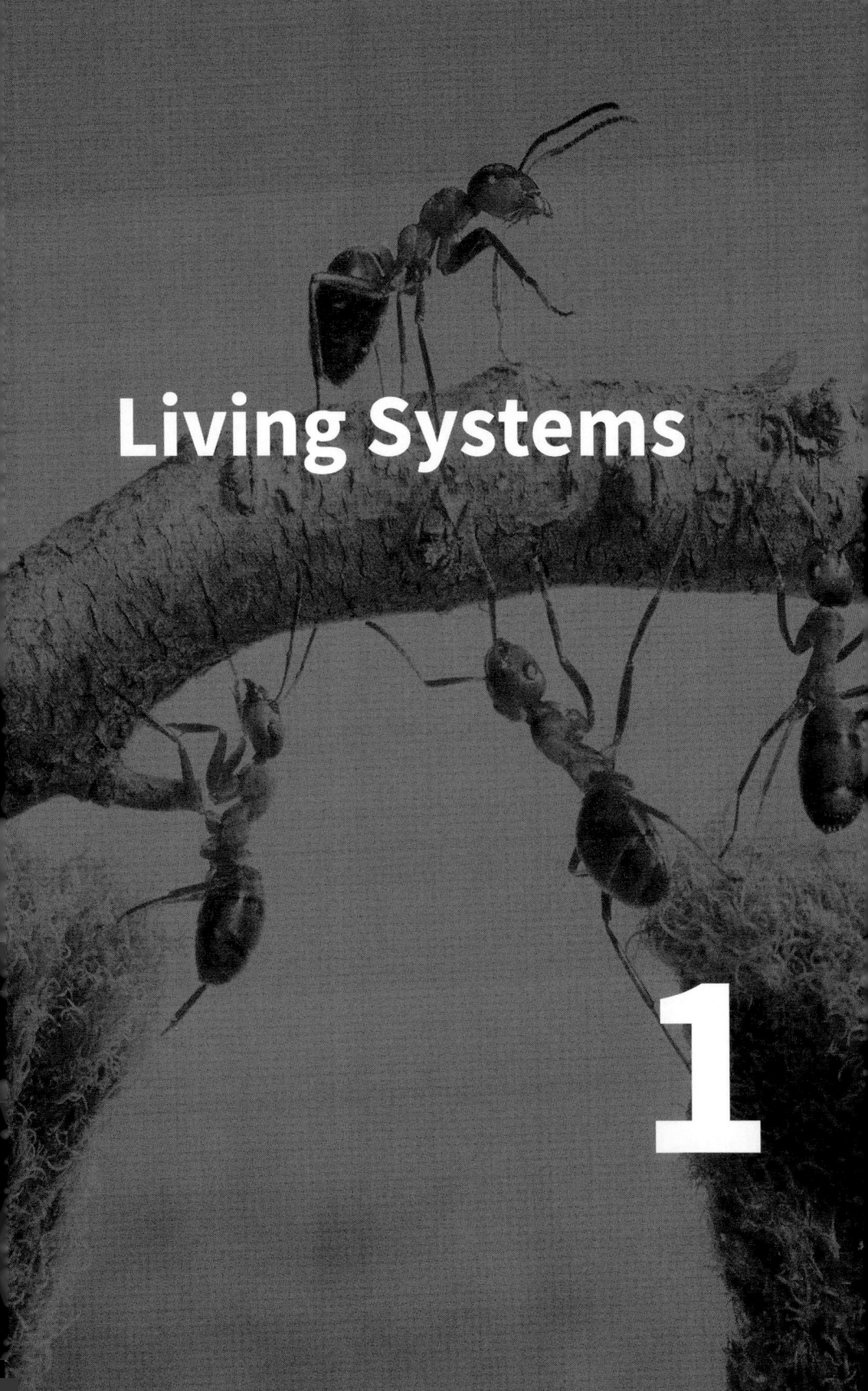

Living Systems

1

- An organisation: a living system
- Characteristics of living systems
- Examples

1.1 An organisation: a living system

" *In the systems approach the properties of the parts can be understood only from the organization of the whole. Accordingly, systems thinking concentrates not on basic building blocks, but on basic principles of organization. Systems thinking is 'contextual', which is the opposite of analytical thinking. Analysis means taking something apart in order to understand it; systems thinking means putting it into the context of a larger whole.* **"**

Fritjof Capra: The Web of Life, 1997

In this book we look at organisations as living systems and at what a consultant can contribute from this perspective. We are not saying it is the only, or the only correct, way of looking. We just state that this point of view, like any other, has its own values and truths. In this first chapter we examine the characteristics of living systems and investigate to what degree, or not, organisations might share these characteristics. Are organisations really living systems? Are they different to other living systems? To do so, we draw on the insights of systems thinking, as described, among others, by Fritjof Capra in The Web of Life. Systems thinking is an approach that looks at the whole. This means not only observing the individual subsystems but, more importantly, the way they interact with each other and with their surrounding systems, and also looking at their places in the whole.

A clarification of the word 'system' is appropriate here. A system is a recognisable identity, consisting of multiple parts. The word system stems from the Greek sustèma, which means to put together, to compose. A living system is an entity, a whole that is in permanent interaction with its surrounding systems and adapts itself to them in order to survive. A certain amount of instability is needed for change, adaptation and innovation and, thus, for survival. But stability is also needed for this entity to exist. A nice example of a living system is a beehive; we'll revisit this idea later in the chapter.

We regard organisations as living systems, because you can recognise them as an entity and because they are always interacting with the surrounding world via multiple interacting parts. And, finally, organisations are marked by both stability and instability and by their focus on continuing their existence. In the following paragraphs we examine the various characteristics of living systems and put them into the context of organisations.

1.2 Characteristics of living systems

" *To understand things systemically, literally means to put them into a context, to establish the nature of their relationships. From the systems point of view, the understanding of life begins with understanding the pattern.* **"**

Fritjof Capra: The Web of Life, 1997

Looking at living systems means looking at the system as a whole, at the relationship between the whole and its parts, and at the parts that are the smallest entities. Moreover, any system is a part of a still-larger whole.

A living system is focussed on survival, in which the parts are in service of the whole. The system itself is embedded again in a bigger entity. This complete field of relationships and dependencies is always in motion. And, amidst this complex mesh of movement and connections, a living system has a self-regulating capacity, through which it creates a permanent equilibrium, both in the balance between its parts and in the relationship between the system and its environment. This equilibrium cannot be other than dynamic, as all that lives is subject to constant change. The most remarkable characteristics of living systems are:

• Living systems are focussed on survival

- Every system is part of a bigger whole
- A system lives by permanent exchange
- The parts of a system are in service of the whole
- The whole is more than the sum of its parts
- The parts display the properties of the whole
- Living systems self-regulate naturally
- Living systems understand the dynamic balance between preservation and exchange

Here we will describe briefly, and in two different ways, each of these characteristics. First we make some general statements about each particular characteristic. Then we 'transfer' the characteristic to organisations by asking in what way is it present in them?

At the end of this chapter we return to the concept of the whole by asking the question, are organisations living systems?

Living systems are focussed on survival

Living systems are focussed on survival, growth, and reproduction. Looking at the world of animals, it strikes us that the single parts, the individual insects or mammals, are not so much focussed on their own survival, they exist in service of the survival of the species. Each individual has a place in the bigger whole. This is especially recognisable when looking at animals that depend upon their group for survival.

Whether it is a flight of geese, a herd of deer, a school of fish or a colony of ants, each individual's behaviour always contributes to the species' best chance of survival.

Are organisations focussed on survival?

Unlike other living systems, organisations have a specific moment when they are founded, when they start up. They have a clear reason for coming into being and a goal that goes further than simply continuing life. An organisation's origin can be an idea, a desire, a social need or a gap in the market. And, subsequently, a new system comes into being, focussed on specific goals: supplying the market with a special service or product, and ensuring the system survives in order to acquire money for the parts of the system. An organisational system can adhere strictly to its original goals, or just move smoothly to and fro in a bigger whole, dynamically adjusting its goals. It is also possible for an organisation to close itself down. When an animal system begins to lose its vitality, its life force, for example because it can no longer gather enough food, it becomes extinct or divides itself into smaller parts. This dividing is visible, for example, when bees hive off to start a new system in a new location. When an organisational system can no longer supply 'food' to its parts, then indeed it can become defunct, it can divide itself. But it can also close itself down and leave the parts with the choice to start a more favourable, new system ... or not.

Every system is part of a bigger whole

> *Many biologists nowadays believe that the whole ecosystem evolves and that this process can really be understood only at the level of the total ecology. ... It suggests that any evolution always is an evolution of a pattern of relations between organisms and their environments. It is the pattern that evolves, not only the separate units that show this pattern. ... If we try to look at organisational ecology from this perspective, we need to understand that organisations and their environments are engaged in a pattern of co-creation, in which the one evokes the other.*

Gareth Morgan: Images of Organization, 1986

Living systems, while distinguishable from their environment, cannot be separated from it. You can distinguish a plant and look at it, but to understand how this plant survives you must consider its environment: the temperature, the amount of sunlight and rain, the soil, the wind, the insects, birds and other animals. By taking into account the environment you understand why this plant has thorns and a bright colour, why it comes into bloom at a given moment, how everything aligns to ensure the seeds will be eaten by birds (that alight exactly when the seeds have ripened), and how the reproduction and continued existence of this plant are interwoven with all kinds of surrounding systems.

Can an organisation be seen separately from its environment?

Of course not, is the obvious answer. The organisation cannot be viewed separately from the bigger whole of customers, cash flow, the buildings and so on. But we are so easily seduced into believing this is possible. How much are you inclined, when reading a newspaper article, or as an employee of a company or an external consultant dealing with a problem, just to zoom in on one branch, one team or one manager? And, conversely, how difficult it is to begin by reviewing the total interaction with the surrounding environment.

A system lives by permanent exchange

Exchange takes place between parts of the system and between the system and the surrounding world. That is the bigger whole with which, in turn, it also forms a system. If, for whatever reason, this exchange stagnates, the system starts to leak life force. All living systems obtain food, water, oxygen and so on from outside the system and convert it into energy. This energy is released by a conversion in which all the internal parts are involved and then waste is set free to be removed. This way there is a continuous flow of exchange.

Organisations and permanent exchange

All kind of things stream into the organisation: goods, people, money, knowledge. Something happens to these things, resulting in a streaming-out of products and services that guarantees a new influx of energy (money). Every organisation is connected with a large and diverse network, where everything is in constant motion. People go in and out, money flows, streams of information spread in all directions; it is fascinating that the vitality of a system seems to be directly related to this characteristic of permanent exchange. The giant panda is an endangered species, particularly because they must eat up to 40 kilos a day of just one kind of bamboo, which enormously increases their vulnerability. Could organisations that depend completely on one kind of energy exchange, for example government funding, also become highly vulnerable?

The parts of a system are in service of the whole

In the world of living systems there is no good or bad behaviour: everyone and everything seems to be programmed to do what best serves survival. Sometimes this needs egoism, sometimes altruism and, sometimes, even self-sacrifice. These are words that lose their familiar meanings. Somehow, everything contributes and judgements are neither appropriate nor useful here. The rabbit that bites its young to death when under threat, seen from the greater whole, is no less functional than the wildebeest protecting their offspring from lions by creating a ring around them.

Are the parts of an organisation in service of the whole?

When an organisational system comes into being, it goes without saying that the parts are in service of the whole and that this contribution is easy and natural. But, over time, parts – divisions, departments, branches, teams, and functions – gradually become increasingly stuck in ensuring their own survival and begin contributing less and less to the whole. You can see this in staff departments, local branches of big companies, a football club's 1st team and the like. Sometimes the smaller units, the employees, seem to be focussed entirely on their own survival.

It appears to be a unique feature of human systems that we are in multiple systems at the same time.

Naturally enough, this causes tension: should my focus be on the survival of my family, my neighbourhood, my country, my department, my organisation, my sports club, my church or another of 'my' systems? So, how humans serve the 'one' whole is not so obvious.

The whole is more than the sum of its parts

❝ *The word community goes as far back as the Indo-European mei, which means 'change' or 'exchange'. Later on mei was combined with the word 'kom', which means with. So arose the Indo-European word kommein: exchanged by all.* **❞**

Peter Senge: The Fifth Discipline –
The Art and Practice of The Learning Organization, 1990

The properties of the whole are more than the sum of the properties of the parts. Moreover, parts can change while the whole does not change. A waterfall or river is often used as an example: not one drop flows back, so the parts are constantly changing, being replaced, yet you still recognise the waterfall. Even when the flow reduces or when it is frozen, from a picture you will still be able to recognize that specific waterfall.

An organisation is more than the sum of its parts

Probably this is the most crucial aspect of organisational systems. It is highly unlikely that every person, ever employed in a particular organisation, was at work at the same moment, yet the organisation still has a recognisable culture, atmosphere and appearance. Even when you return to your old school after fifteen years and all the teachers have been replaced, you still recognise it. Parts are being sold, mergers take place, people move in and on, sites, products and services change and still company A keeps its character and personality and will be recognised as company A. If your approach to changing an organisation's culture is by bringing in new blood (from outside the system), can that ever be successful? Does a system really, fundamentally, change when all its people have been replaced?

The parts display the properties of the whole

This means that the properties of the parts only can be understood in the context of the whole. Although no leaf is the same, every leaf of a beech tree is identifiable as a beech leaf. And although no two beech trees are the same, every tree of this species is identifiable as being a beech.

The parts show the properties of the organisation as a whole

Obviously the staff stick to the many familiar rituals that belong so much to their company or department. The language, the clothing, the way of walking, the jokes, the volume with which one speaks, the distance people keep between each other; something from the bigger whole is reflected in every mode of expression. You can see all of these traits at, for example, a conference centre, in the way people approach the table that is set for their company. Observe the supporters at a football match and you will see individuals belonging to a greater whole.

Shouting, calling and singing is conduct that is a part of that bigger whole. It is the kind of behaviour that the same people would not easily show in their work systems. Whenever an attempt is made to change the culture of an organisation, exclusively by training the separate parts, then the character of the organisation is being ignored. A culture where the parts do not feel accountable to the whole will not change by just changing the parts (for example, by training some staff in giving effective feedback).

Living systems self-regulate naturally

❝ *Out of chaos often arises life, out of order habits.* **❞**

Henry Brooks Adams, American historian, 1838-1918

Living systems self-regulate naturally. This self-regulation cares for the system by responding to any change, without losing its sense of self. The concept emanates from the science of physiology, where the term homeostasis is used to mean self-regulation. It refers to the ability of humans and animals to keep their internal environment, their own body, stable and relatively constant – temperature, for example – while the external environment, the surroundings where the organism lives, is in constant change. Homeostasis utilises various internal control systems and the same applies to other living systems.

Self-regulation functions in protection of the whole. It powers the dynamic equilibrium between preservation and exchange, and is the source of the signals and symptoms the system shows when its equilibrium is disturbed. Self-regulation ensures a new and viable balance is found between stability and instability and warns when the balance is in danger.

Organisations and self-regulation

Self-regulation is the driving force behind survival. The systemic approach focusses, in particular, on exploring this self-regulation. Sometimes employees, departments or organisations exhibit difficult, contradictory or even destructive behaviour. Assuming that the organisation is a living system, focussed on survival, it could be that it is the self-regulating force that initiates these behaviours – in favour of the system as a whole.

Living systems understand the dynamic balance between preservation and exchange

> **"** *In a human body, new bone is constantly being produced by bone-creating cells called osteoblasts. At the same time, the bone is broken off by osteoclasts. So the bone is a dynamic tissue that is continuously being renewed. Most bone illnesses are the result of a disturbance in the balance between the making and braking down of the bone.* **"**
>
> *Dr Jojanneke Jukes: University of Twente*

A living system is like an art mobile. When anything changes, anywhere in the balance of the whole, then all the parts automatically respond.

Any living system needs this exchange with its surrounding systems as much as it needs stability and the preservation of identity and individuality. The right mix between these factors reinforces the character and viability of the system.

Exchange creates possibilities for change, growth and adaptation. If exchange stops, the system will, bit by bit, reduce in vitality until, eventually, it dies. However, a system, focussed too much on exchanging and adapting to other systems, will lose its identity and 'melt' into other systems.

The forces of preservation and stability take care of what is vital to the system. If stability decreases, the balance tips towards instability; the system risks either falling apart or being totally absorbed by another system. A system focussed too much on preservation and stability becomes rigid, sealed off from the outside world and, finally, as a result, loses its right to continue: it dies away. There is the ever-present question of what balance between preservation and exchange provides the system with the vitality it needs.

In the course of history, those species unable to adapt fast enough to changes in their environment became extinct. Reacting too quickly can also create problems. Identity, individuality and access to accumulated experience might well come with risk. Wild animals raised by humans sometimes adapt so well that they can no longer survive in the wild. They do not know the risks or survival techniques and their own kind no longer recognises them as 'one of their own'. We see this, for example, with orca whales that have been saved, or used, by humans.

Organisations and dynamic tension between preservation and growth

Two regulating forces are at work in the creation and development of organisational systems. One force is focussed on maintaining internal cohesion, taking care of preserving individuality and identity, of access to the accumulated experience and on holding the parts together.

Often this force is connected to the past, the roots, the origin and the experiences. The system's other force focusses on exchange. It causes renewal by growing, pruning and adapting and takes care of the raison d'être of this system, now and in the future, by permanent interaction with the outside world. Whereas the force of preservation and stability makes the organisation stand on its own two feet, so to speak, and shapes it into a recognizable entity, the force of exchange determines where and how this organisation continuously finds its own place in the bigger whole.

In organisations some functions (places), are more connected with preservation, others more with exchange. Account managers work on the meeting-edges of their own and other organisations, as a result they are focussed on renewal and adapting to the outside world. Production units, for example, are focussed on the preservation of quality and continuity by the best use of existing production lines. By nature they are more connected to internal processes and preservation. Often these two 'sides' find it difficult to acknowledge each other's value and easily find themselves in a conflict where the 'forces' of preservation are seen as being in a rut, while the 'forces' of renewal are seen to support dangerous action that threatens the system's continuity.

In some organisations the present knowledge (preservation) disappears from the system too quickly, because all the attention is focussed on the new (growth). Many such organisations forced employees into early retirement (pruning) only to have to re-employ them, as they possessed knowledge that was still crucial to the system: this is self-regulation at work, finding a new balance.

Understanding 'preservation and growth'

The feeling, inherent in these two systemic forces, is more important than the precise meaning. So here are two groups of words that resonate more with one or the other.

Preservation	Exchange
Cohesion	Renewal
Inward Focus	Flexibility
Stability	Instability
Group Feeling	Outward Focus
Predictability	Changeable
Continuity	Fluctuation
Structure	Adaptation
Everyone a place and task	Adopting new ways & methods
Streamlining	Taking risks
Consolidating	Reinventing the wheel
Rigidity	Making new connections
Bureaucracy	Falling apart
Isolation	Chaos
Cannot get on with the outside world	Proliferation

The concept of preservation seems to fit easily with nature, and growth with economics. How would it be if we looked at economic preservation and growth in the context of nature? Some political parties, for example, can appear to be more engaged by growth (of prosperity, companies, the economy) while others with preservation (of the health care system, employment, the environment). This can easily lead to misunderstandings and a sense of being 'against' the other. How would it be if all parties acknowledged the value, to the whole, of both forces?

An organisation: a living system

We have seen that organisations are essentially the same as other living systems. They function, too, via permanent exchange, self-regulation and dynamic balance and live nested within a bigger whole. A fundamental difference between organisational systems and other living systems, however, is that organisations are not necessarily focussed on survival. What is also clearly evident is that the parts are in service of the whole in a very different way: because people – after all it is they that populate organisations – are, simultaneously, parts of multiple systems and so cannot be completely in service of just one system. Every person belongs to a family – or private system – and then to other systems such as their sports club, groups of friends or their church (perhaps). Probably there is no automatic impulse to connect, with all one's heart, to just one system, as there are multiple systems and therefore multiple ways of connecting and surviving. For the people system this multiplicity might have contributed to the survival of the species, but also has consequences for the degree of individual connection and devotion to each system. This means organisations and their populations must consciously rebuild this commitment and devotion again and again.

1.3 Examples

- What kind of balance strengthens the whole?
- The giant panda: a system at its end?
- The beehive as a system

What kind of balance strengthens the whole?

More central of more connected with parts?

Imagine an HR function. It is a part of a central organisation, but most of the HR personnel work at one of the offices of the five divisions, spread across the country. The divisional directors like this construction: they have professional HR staff at hand, who operate flexibly and know exactly what 'their own' division needs. The HR manager is not so happy: there is a lack of consistency across decision making in each division. What is common practice in one division is completely unacceptable in another. HR staff members do not easily replace each other during vacations or sick leave; something you could expect if they all worked in one location.

HR staff members are happy with their freedom, and enjoy responsibility combined with independence and recognition of their professionalism by their 'individual' divisions. But they lack a sense of togetherness with their colleagues: they miss the daily exchange, helping and supporting each other. The question is, what is the added value of combining all five divisional HR functions together in one physical location? Currently, each HR staff member reports directly to his divisional director.

This HR system is very open, focussed on maximum exchange with the outside world and has lots of innovation energy. It is quite possible that its external focus is so great that, in the end, it merges with the other system, the divisional. There is also the question of which system has priority: the HR system – or the divisional system –, and which choice – in the end – would most reinforce the greater whole, the organisation. The HR personnel would like more internal cohesion. However the question remains … are they prepared to pay the price for this? Willing to lose some of their freedom and flexibility, their focus on their 'own' divisions.

SIEBKE KAAT AND ANTON DE KROON

The giant panda: a system at its end?

The giant panda

The giant panda is a descendent of the order of predators, but has evolved into a plant eater. Its food is, almost entirely, a particular species of bamboo that blooms irregularly (the frequency varies from three to 150 years) and then dies. In 1975, huge areas of bamboo in the Chinese forests vanished due to habitat fragmentation and unsustainable development, indirectly causing the deaths of more than 100 pandas. Even when there is enough (of the right) bamboo the panda still has a significant problem: his intestines are still adapted to a carnivorous diet and so he digests bamboo with some difficulty. On top of this, this bamboo has a low nutrient content and the majority of the bamboo consumed exits the panda's intestinal tract undigested. In order to survive, a panda needs to eat nine to fourteen kilos of bamboo every day, at an average of one kilo per hour.

The giant panda is an endangered species. One reason is the fact that it eats mainly bamboo, while the bamboo supply, for various reasons, is shrinking. Another reason is that panda reproduction is difficult. The female is fertile only once a year – for just three days. She is very selective and easily rejects potential partners. Although pandas are being bred in captivity, mating is a complicated and slow process, partly due to the males having weak libidos. Therefore, in zoos, they get special treatment: panda pornography to stimulate their desire and food provided on high poles to strengthen their hind legs. This 'training' is a necessity for real mating, as it allows the males to stand on their hind legs for long enough to mate.

Often twins are born, but usually only one survives because the mother only feeds one baby. New-born pandas are very vulnerable: the babies stay with their mothers for three years, during which time the females do not mate, so reproduction is, again, limited.

Pandas are generally perceived as being very 'cute' due to the striking pattern of their fur, especially on their faces, and their soft appearance. It is not surprising that the World Wildlife Fund has chosen the panda as its mascot and symbol.

The panda and us

What happens to us when we meet a (any) system in terminal decline, the ending of which is made more likely by our involvement. What is it that we really want to save? Our need to control? Our personal concept of an honest, makeable world? Do we want to pay off our debts? Or do we want to keep everything just as it was when we were born?

For what reason, when some systems end, do we say *"Fortunately, it is over."* Yet with another imminent ending we do our utmost to keep the system alive, even though it might no longer have meaning or purpose. We humans easily set ourselves up as super regulators, protecting one and destroying the other. Animals threatened with extinction are bred in zoos, while we want to eradicate malaria-carrying mosquitos. Can we accept that the keys to preservation and change are not in our hands? Can we learn to see ourselves as parts of a bigger whole? Or, in our own minds, are we the bigger whole that gives all other parts their places?

What happens to people when an organisational system reaches the end of its time? How do societies, customers, shareholders, employees, workers' councils, management, HR staff and local communities react? Which group focusses on preservation, looking for ways to care for the organisation, just as we do for the panda in captivity? Imagine a system that, for many reasons, is no longer viable. Who are more likely to accept the pruning and dying-off, and who see the dying-off process as an opportunity for something else to come into bloom?

The beehive as a system

The beehive

The beehive is an impressive example of preservation and renewal maintained in dynamic balance, achieved via self-regulation of the system: the hive and the colony becoming almost a single entity. And, as this is in service of the whole, it might even cost individuals their lives. A bee lives in a hive, which can be seen as a system. At its head are the workers. Collectively, it is they that rule the hive, not the queen.

SIEBKE KAAT AND ANTON DE KROON

They allow and support the presence of one queen in the hive. She enjoys a pampered existence, because the life of the hive depends on her. When the old queen's egg-production begins to decrease, or she produces increasing numbers of unfertilised eggs, the worker bees will begin the process of making a new queen. First they build a number of larger cells known as queen cups. From eggs between one and three days old, the workers choose the most beautiful and place them in the queen cups. From the very beginning, the larvae from these eggs get special treatment: more food, better food and more often. They are fed on Royal Jelly secreted by the worker bees. Due to this food a queen comes into being. The old queen will leave, around seven days before the new queen emerges from her cell, accompanied by about half of the hive, in a process called swarming.

If there are multiple 'new' queens some will also leave by swarming but, at a certain time, the remaining virgin queen will kill the rest of the queen larvae. Now her nuptial flight begins. She shoots up into the air pursued by drones from her own hive and from near and far, hurrying to sacrifice themselves for the greater whole. The first to get to the queen mates with her in the air. In the embrace the drone loses his genital organ, causing his death. Other drones try their luck too. When she has been fertilized by up to 15 drones she possesses enough sperm cells for the rest of her life. The unsuccessful drones return to their hives.

In August the worker bees chase the drones away from the hive. Any drones that try to return will be chased away or killed. Slaughtering of the drones occurs because the colony needs all the honey it has for hibernating; once a virgin queen is inseminated, the drones have no other function that serves the hive as a whole.

Self-regulation in service of the whole

Once a part's function becomes redundant the system separates from it (the drones). When a part's function only decreases (the queen growing older and weakening the whole), self-regulation ensures preservation via the process of creating a new queen.

Coherence and exchange

There is no single leader in the bee system: it consists of about 50,000 short-living individuals. There is, indeed, a strict order in which every bee has its place. This prevents chaos and anarchy and causes the system to be both stable and flexible. For the preservation of the whole, it is not useful if all the bees, whose task it is to fly out every morning to search for food, actually leave the hive. Therefore only the searcher bees go exploring. This makes sense only if, on their return, they have ways to communicate to the others. They convey the important information they have gathered via three dances: a different dance for each different kind of food they find. This way they exchange information about the smell, taste, distance and direction of the food source. This way the preservation of the whole and both the internal and external exchange are in a beautiful balance.

Self-regulation and vitality

Over the last few years, mortality among domesticated hives of honeybees has increased dramatically and unnaturally. The question is whether humans have contributed to disturbing the vitality of these systems. Not only by changing the environment through the use of insecticides, but also by deliberately creating large hives with characteristics that are favourable for the apiarists (beekeepers) rather than the bees. Characteristics that include a limited need for swarming, low aggression and high honey production. The flight of the drones – where chance or some higher wisdom determines which drones fertilise the queen – is often replaced by controlled mating, where mankind intervenes for his own benefit. Probably, we have constricted natural self-regulation by too much intervention, resulting in a less-vital system.

What organisations can learn from bees

For the bees there is a time of contributing to the whole and a time of being surplus; for the queen, just as for the drones.

SIEBKE KAAT AND ANTON DE KROON

What about the employees and departments of an organisation? When can you still contribute and when is there no longer a place for you? And how could this be made visible on a regular basis? What happens to the organisation – as a whole – when certain departments, personnel and functions have gone? What happens to the system's vitality when these kinds of questions may no longer be asked? Often they are only voiced when cutbacks are planned. For example, when the outside world makes it painfully clear that, for too long, self-regulation by the system has been ineffective, dangerously disturbing its balance. And yes, then, searching, little by little, for a new balance usually doesn't happen. In its place comes one big seismic event that leads to a new balance, but one that carries the risk of becoming rigid quite quickly, instead of maintaining its dynamism.

At first sight there might appear to be no hierarchy among bees. But every individual bee has a duty for the whole and a place in the whole.

How could we create and manage something similar within an organisational system? Clearly it seems necessary that every part is conscious that it is a part of a larger whole. The contribution of a part can only be understood in and from the larger whole; not the other way round. There are many examples of small, young organisations, populated with highly-educated professionals, that have started life this way with great success. In these organisations nobody has a title, everyone contributes to the whole, and each chooses what should be his salary, reflecting how he values his contribution to the whole.

The workers notice their queen's reducing vitality and, motivated by the interests of the hive, they act accordingly.

Who are the first to recognise that an organisation is losing strength? Those inside or outside the organisation? In high or low positions? New arrivals or long-term employees?

Controlled mating means determining in advance what characteristics you desire in your population.

Shouldn't we be happy that it will never be certain that an applicant has the qualities we 'need'? Perhaps the real vitality lies in what we do not know about him or her.

(Our thanks to Els Wittens, beekeeper at the Beehive Association of Ede, the Netherlands.)

The background to the systemic approach

2

- Introduction

- Systemic phenomenology

- Phenomenology: perception without judgement

- Gestalt therapy: becoming aware

- Insights from family systems

- Family and organisational constellations

- Other influences

- Summary

2.1 Introduction

Systems thinking, system-oriented and systemic are frequently used, but mixed-up notions. In this chapter we discuss how the systemic approach evolved from systems thinking, as we described in the previous chapter. We start with the origin of the word systemic, after which we describe the avenues of thought and the disciplines that fed and influenced the systemic approach. As working systemically with organisational systems is quite new, we should expect that its development will accelerate in the future.

2.2 Systemic phenomenology

What we call the systemic approach is, on the one hand, a method arising from systems thinking – as discussed in the previous chapter – and, on the other hand, one that has its roots in phenomenology. It seems appropriate to call it the systemic-phenomenological approach, usually shortened to the systemic approach. We use this term, conscious that it is this precise combination of knowledge about living systems and learning from the phenomena – as they are revealed – that leads us towards completely new insights about systems.

2.3 Phenomenology: perception without judgement

Phenomenology is a method in philosophy that wants to see and understand phenomena exactly as they are revealed to us. The founder, Edmund Husserl (1859 – 1938), pointed-out that our tendency to rationalise can make us easily overlook an obvious source of information: the world as it appears in front of us and what we come to know via our direct and indirect intuitive perception of all that shows itself to us. Phenomenology calls on us to see the world without judgement, without any interpretation. Phenomenology adds our open and immediate perception as a new source of knowledge.

The systemic approach distinguishes itself by its phenomenological attitude. This implies a willingness to put aside all your knowledge about organisations and systems and to look only at what arises. It means to let go of all you have learned about connections and fulfilling needs. To refrain from imposing a model onto the world but, again and again, to only see the world as it is. The most you might bring are some cautious hypotheses, carried over from previous experience and knowledge of systems.

One of the characteristics of living systems is that the whole is mirrored in the parts. By looking, without bias, at the phenomena in a part, you receive information about the whole.

2.4 Gestalt therapy: becoming aware

Gestalt therapy began when Fritz Perls (1893-1970) took, as his point of departure, perception in the here-and-now. He called it awareness and this phenomenon – of immediate registration of all perceptions – developed from a side interest into the main issue. In this form of therapy, both client and therapist are challenged to register and name what happens to each of them in their mutual contact.

When both phenomenological perception and one's sensations are in the foreground, accepted knowledge about organisational systems can be enriched with insights into the unique ways in which any specific living system (organisation) is reacting.

This is an open way of being and corresponds with what C. Otto Schar- mer describes, in Theory U, as presencing: seeing from the source. In this absolutely open attitude it is not about searching for something, but notic- ing what shows itself.

Therefore, the systemic approach mainly suggests in which direction to look, in order to get a better understanding of what is going on in an organisation. And remember, every organisation is a unique system, with a unique history, in a unique environment.

2.5 Insights from family systems

Systems thinking has been successfully applied to family therapy and this has enriched our knowledge of how human systems function. Iván Böször- ményi-Nagy's (1920-2007) contextual therapy made an important contri- bution by identifying how similar patterns can appear in multiple gen- erations. He saw the huge, unconscious loyalty of children to their par- ents and gained insight into the ways people continuously protect and re- store the balance of taking and giving. The systems therapist Virginia Satir (1916-1988) was one of the first to work with a whole family as her client system. She was looking for self-healing forces and made family members aware of patterns that persist through generations. Salvador Minuchin also deserves a mention here: his structural family therapy does not fo- cus on removing a symptom, but on changing the structure in the family, so giving the symptom the chance to disappear. He directed attention to the hierarchies within systems and distinguished several subsystems. Sig- mund Freud and later Carl Jung were the first to recognise the role of the unconscious in steering human behaviour. Many other therapists, scien- tists and movements have, directly or indirectly, influenced current ways of thinking and working with family systems.

New insights about human systems, from various sources, continue to find a place in the systemic approach to organisations:

- Patterns can cross generations.

- People act in accordance with loyalties of which they are not con- scious.

- People have an unerring feeling for the balance between taking and giving.

- The more the system as a whole is reinforced, the more the individual members can solve their own problems.

- The structure of the system – within which is defined who belongs to which subsystem, and which place is available for every subsystem – is an important influence on the vitality of the system.

2.6 Family and organisational constellations

Bert Hellinger founded the systemic-phenomenological approach. He brought together his knowledge and experience of phenomenology, Gestalt and systems therapy into the method we now know as family constellations. He chooses individuals, at random, to represent family members and he invites his clients to place them in the room in relationship to each other: this makes it possible to see many generations at the same time. He looks and feels into this field, employing all his senses and awareness, and asks himself: *"What is showing itself here? What might be the issue in this system?"* When facilitating a constellation, the phenomenological approach and utilising direct perception are inextricably connected with knowledge of (human) systems.

Hellinger's modus operandi was embraced by people from many fields, developing individual approaches to the constellations method and enlarging our understanding of human systems. In 1995 Hellinger set up the first organisational constellation, in response to a question from the German psychiatrist Gunthard Weber. Hellinger immediately saw the potential of organisational constellations but, at that time, felt more comfortable with family constellations. So he asked Weber to take on the development of organisational constellations. He did so, with great energy and enthusiasm, and began using the word systemic. The work began to gain recognition in Germany, where Matthias Varga von Kibéd and Ilsa Sparrer made significant contributions to its development. Jan Jacob Stam brought the systemic-phenomenological approach and constellations to the Netherlands and continues to develop this approach through workshops and training courses around the world and by bringing innovative thinkers and practitioners to the Netherlands.

2.7 Other influences

The systemic-phenomenological approach to organisations is becoming more and more a discipline in itself. It clarifies that working systemically is not exactly the same as using constellations and that patterns specific to organisational systems can be distinguished. This discipline benefits from its dialogue with the field of change and transformation. Thought leaders in this field include Karl Weick, who brought into view the irrational layers of organisations and Otto Scharmer, Joseph Jaworski, Peter Senge, Arawana Hayashi et al. who constantly search for ways and methods of in-depth collective change.

There is a healthy symbiosis between this larger field of knowledge and expertise and the systemic-phenomenological approach, which enriches and renews it.

2.8 Summary

The systemic approach has three clear elements.

- Phenomenology: perceiving, without judgement, the phenomena and sensations as they arise;

- Knowledge of organisational systems: fundamental needs and patterns;

- Attitude of the consultant: focussed on reinforcing the vitality of the system(s).

In the next chapter we'll discuss the fundamental needs of organisational systems, and then we'll describe how to apply this knowledge as a consultant and what is the inner attitude it asks from you.

Organisational systems

3

- Introduction

- Five fundamental needs

- Self-regulation

- Origin

- History

- Belonging

- Order

- Balance

- Patterns

3.1 Introduction

So far we have explored the characteristics of living systems and the origin of the systemic approach. Now we shall look more closely at organisational systems and, specifically, what they need to maintain vitality.

We distinguish five fundamental needs of organisational systems. The degree to which these needs are being met determines the system's vitality. These needs are not unique to organisations; they exist in other living systems such as families. But here we focus on organisations. Many of these basic needs have become evident in the work with organisational constellations. But we are also seeing them appear more and more when we work directly with organisations, or parts of them, without using constellations. So, what we describe is our actual experience, confirmed by many others; it does not have its origins in scientific theory. We suggest the systemic approach as a hypothesis and invite you to explore it when you are working with an organisation and something arises that needs a particular kind of attention.

First we will describe the basic needs, followed by an exploration of how the system self-regulates. This chapter wraps up by looking at common patterns that can be seen in an organisation when one or more fundamental needs are not adequately fulfilled.

3.2 Five fundamental needs

Organisations are potent and truly alive when each of the following needs is met:

- The origin must be recognised as the starting point.
- Acknowledgement of the history is the basis for the present.
- All that belongs has the right to be a part.
- In the order of the whole each part has its own place.
- There is a fair balance between taking and giving.

The origin must be recognised as the starting point

An organisation always has a beginning. This beginning is the foundation on which all the rest is built, even if additional foundations are added later. The origin is connected to the original reasons for coming into being. Organisational systems, unlike other living systems, are not just focussed on survival. Organisations and their parts (such as departments and divisions) gain vitality by giving recognition to their original raison d'être. It is this origin, in its specific context, that made the organisation what it is now. That is why it is important that, in some way, there is always recognition in an organisation for how it started and for those who started it: the founders. What was the reason for founding the system? What intention or wish was behind the decision? What question, need or necessity was answered or met through creating the organisation? What were the values that drove its creators? To whom or what did the organisation begin supplying products or services?

When you start digging around the origin of an organisation, the answers lead you to its roots. Witnessing these and seeing their value, even if the organisation has changed its direction, feeds and adds vitality to the organisation in the present.

It is because of its particular origin that this particular system exists now, and that everything to do with this system is the way it is now.

Acknowledgment of the history is the basis for the present

A second fundamental need is that the history, all of it, is 'seen' completely and accepted as being a real part of the organisation. This means that nothing that happened during the life of the organisation can be ignored, hidden or minimised.

What occurred as the organisation developed? Are there scratches on its soul, for example, because people, departments or even products have disappeared without their contributions being acknowledged? Has the organisation remained true to its original values? What did it lose on the way, what did it add? Did the gains correspond with the original intentions and values, or do they fit poorly into the system?

Whatever happened, happened: the good and the bad together have made the organisation what it is now; it all belongs with the organisation.

All that belongs has the right to be a part

The third basic need is that everything that is a part of the organisation has a right to be visible and to be considered.

Large or small, important or unimportant, all the parts that make the organisation whole must be seen. Perhaps this is so important because individual elements can belong to many different (sub)systems at the same time. When a part is not seen, the cohesion, the internal stability of the system, is diminished.

Can we see everything and everyone who currently belongs to the system? Are there elements, values, people, functions or departments that are being ignored, even though they do belong? For example, do long-term-sick employees still belong? Or trainees? Or the department that will no longer exist one year from now? Or the new subsidiary, which has only a skeleton staff at the moment, does it belong to the organisation? Have all the new elements received the recognition and place they deserve?

In the order of the whole each part has its own place

An organisation is not just an assembling of loose parts, in any order. Everything must have its own, appropriate place; this is the next fundamental need.

What is the quality and nature of the inner cohesion between functions, teams and products? Does everything and everybody have a place, one that allows them to contribute appropriately to the whole system? Is everyone's place in the order clear? Are there any missing places, missing elements? Do some places have more than one occupant? Do some take too much or too little space? Is everybody in their own place? Or someone else's? Do we say a proper goodbye to things that no longer have a rightful place?

In many other living systems, you understand immediately who the leader is. In organisational systems it is just as necessary for this to be clear but, even when we have an organisation chart to guide us, there can still be doubts about exactly the right order.

There is a fair balance between taking and giving

When there is balance in taking and giving, between the different departments within an organisation and with the organisation and the outside world, the organisation is solid and flexible. Is there balance in what the different officials, teams and departments take from and give to the organisation?

How does exchange go between the customers, clients, patients and the organisation? What is rewarded? How is imbalance addressed? Are people falling ill, doing poor quality work or quitting their jobs. Are they cheating and committing fraud? Are there people who give too much? Are there people who feel the urge to take back, in order to restore balance?

A healthy balance is palpable. Around the pivot point of the balance you find liveliness, satisfaction, creativity; no resentment or envy. A healthy balance reflects a healthy equilibrium between retention and exchange.

Contrary to the usual expression give and take, we reverse the order. Life begins with taking and only after taking can you start giving. You accept a job, a function; the organisation accepts you, the candidate. Then the exchange of taking and giving begins.

To summarise: the organisation is most powerful and vital when these five fundamental needs are fully met. Only then are both cohesion and exchange possible. Ignoring one or more of these needs diminishes energy and flexibility and it becomes impossible to face evolving circumstances and new challenges. Then self-regulation begins, the system provides itself with what it needs and the symptoms of this response become visible. Identifying the causes behind the symptoms is the basis of the systemic approach.

3.3 Self-regulation

>   **"** *Confusion is a word we have invented for an order which is not yet understood.* **"**
>
>   *Henry Miller: American author, 1891-1980*

The self-regulating ability of a living system ensures that reactions occur if there is a disruption that threatens the vitality of the system. We are all familiar with how we start sweating when the environment is very hot. This reaction (sweating) is both a warning signal and a recovery response. The signal is: mind the heat. The recovery is that sweating cools you off. In organisations too, self-regulation occurs, accompanied by signal and recovery. However, this self-regulation can have a big influence on human behaviour inside the organisation and people are not always aware of this. Usually, in fact, they haven't a clue that the system is 'using' them and that, in one way or another, they are working for the benefit of the greater whole. Just as sweat glands don't know that they are being used by and for the human system, or elephants don't know that by protecting their babies they are also serving the survival of the group. The parts are being directed by the whole. These signal and recovery reactions are automatic responses to the system going out of balance and losing strength due to one or more of the five needs no longer being adequately met.

A system's capacity for self-regulation is based upon using discrete parts of that same system. People, teams, functions or other parts of the whole might unconsciously display behaviour that we consider as problematic, but that we can learn to see as highlighting something, crucial to the system's vitality, that needs attention.

We call this unconscious loyalty. The systemic approach tries to understand, precisely, to what the people are loyal; it searches for what self-regulation is trying to rebalance. This way of looking can open new perspectives, especially when particular behaviours are difficult to explain. It focusses one's attention on the five basic needs through this question: is there something wrong or missing to which this specific behaviour is trying to draw attention?

Unconscious loyalty

When a leader is dismissed without explanation, his team could remain unconsciously loyal to him or her. This means they give the newcomer no chance. When you look at this in a systemic way, these employees are making a positive contribution.

All the time that the team is refusing the new leader, the system is asking for attention for the second fundamental need: acknowledgement of its history. In this particular case, recognition of the former leader's contribution, even if there was good reason to fire him.

If the contribution is honoured, the team are free to accept the new leader and the system can calm down. Then the symptom has done its job: what was systemically wrong and made it weak, has been repaired.

3.4 Origin

The origin must be seen as the starting point.

> **"** *The origin of all things is small (Omnia rerum parva sunt).* **"**
>
> *Marcus Tullius Cicero, 106–43 B.C.*

- Reason to come into being
- Guiding principles in an organisation
- Questions to explore the origin

Reason to come into being

A living system that no longer knows from where it originates is, at best, a knight-errant. It feels something noble inside, but is without direction.

When the organisation loses sight of its origin, this has consequences for the vitality of the whole. People connect with an organisation. And this is more than the function, the mission and the people present. The organisation has an origin and many links, in which any employee, albeit perhaps temporarily, is one of them. Where do you belong if there is no attention to the original purpose, the wish, the target group or the reason to come into being? In which chain are you then a link?

The origin includes various aspects like the immediate cause, the motives, the wish, the ideal. Someone was instrumental in laying the foundations upon which the organisation could grow. Something was the reason for coming into existence. Something gave birth to a spark that became a flame. What did not yet exist was given shape and substance.

Paying attention to these factors, rather than taking them for granted, places the current reality side by side with the original reality. Doing so can, all of a sudden, restore the connection; something of the former passion is felt again and the present organisation and its goals are nourished once more. Sometimes the reasons behind certain behaviours or choices

– why things are as they are – can become perfectly clear. At an unconscious level, certain elements of the system remain loyal to the basic need, which, at present, is not being seen and honoured enough by the whole of the organisation.

Attention to the origin goes together very well with renewal and change of direction. This asking for attention is a plea to know and honour the roots of the organisation and, subsequently, either to go in the same direction or to change track in an appropriate way. Without proper acknowledgement there can be no parting of the ways. Without the founder and the original raison d'être, this organisation would not be. If, in the beginning, the organisation had not had a reason to exist, it could not exist now. This is a fundamental truth and, one way or the other, this is always noticeable, no matter how many decades and mergers later. It is valuable.

By seeing it, by listening to how it resonates and by recognising its value, it can be present in a supportive way. What gets attention no longer has to scream for it.

Development since the origin

In a large firm, from the very beginning, the Department of Training, Education and Organisational Development offered training programs for the staff. This required that the department knew the needs of the staff and offered programs accordingly.

Many years later the department has developed into three teams according to the three tasks of Training, Education and Organisational Development. However, within the firm, almost everyone still refers to all three as 'education'. The consultants, who are tasked with change programs, have difficulty finding their place. For the consultants attached to the Organisational Development Team it is hard to be continuously associated with 'education'. It is obvious that there are very structured programs, not only for training courses and educational programs, but also for meetings about reflection, strategy and teamwork, which the consultant must facilitate. Everything from the planning of a session through to the goals, means and methods are clearly set out. All this occurs as a result of the consultants' loyalty to the origin, even when they want to free themselves from it. How could a team like this be positioned? Here's a try:

"We were Educators, that is why we were able to see across the whole organisation and to have a very good idea of what was going on.

As educators we were used to thinking and working with meticulously-designed teaching plans and we gladly accepted responsibility for the personal development of individual employees. Now we have become consultants – with an excellent understanding of the whole organisation and what is going on in it – and we are the ones who help you to design a step-by-step plan for your organisation's development."

Imagine this team saying "This is what we are now." *The organisation would respond with* "But you were educators". *This perception of them keeps them trapped in their old clothes until the origin receives appropriate recognition.*

Connected with the reason for existence

Albert Heijn, a well-known Dutch grocer, turned the company his grandfather founded into a global success. During the forty years that he led the group he grew its value from € 14 million to € 8 billion.

He always asked the question, "Why should we do this?" Finding the answer to that question was related to the reason for existence of the supermarket chain that carries his name. He had one, simple mission: to improve the life of the housewife. This was his guideline for every choice made. For his farewell he donated to the company a statue of a woman carrying two shopping bags … It was his own answer to his original question, "Why?". The inscription on the pedestal reads "So that we do not forget for whom we work."

After the merger

A housing corporation, the product of many mergers, is aware of the fact that all its predecessors had their focus on affordable housing for people with low incomes. Some of these organisations had already ex-

*isted for more than 100 years, sometimes created by a church, or by po-
litical engagement, or having another origin. It is respectful to stand
still for a moment and take in these facts. And, by doing so, to give
an extra impulse to the current policy that, perhaps now in a different
way, is still focussed on affordable housing for people with low incomes.
Having the awareness, as an employee, that you are standing in a long
chain reaching right back to the roots of the organisation, gives creative
strength to one's duties.*

Guiding principles in an organisation

For every organisation there was one particular moment to come into being. There were needs in the outside world and the organisation, somehow, could fulfil them. If it had not done so, it would have been extinct
long ago. It is that simple. One way or another this reason-to-come-into-
existence steers how people act within the organisation. Often this happens unconsciously. We call this mechanism the guiding principle. It gives
strength and direction. It is something completely different from vision
and mission. They are devised and formulated to manage the organisation. Guiding principles exist simply because they were incorporated in
the basis of a living system.

What are we here for?

*Traditionally, the Dutch police force undertook some basic tasks, like at-
tending incidents, tracing criminals, conducting surveillance. As a guiding principle we could call this 'enforcing'. Little by little, more goals
and tasks were added, for example those focussed on prevention. Let
us say that enforcement and prevention are the two guiding principles
within the police – this is an oversimplification, but helpful as a way of
explaining – then this asks for clarity about which principle comes first.
Before you know it, a struggle between the principles might arise, in
which some part of the organisation is loyal to one principle and another part to the other principle, until the organisation is forced to clarify
its current reason for existence and how the guiding principles fit with*

it. Not being clear about which is the prime guiding principle can man-
ifest itself in many different ways. For example, in stress around deci-
sions about budget and resource allocation, but also in the question
of how to present oneself to the outside world. Is the policeman your
best friend? Or does this erode the enforcement principle? If so, then
the system will react by drawing attention to whichever of the guiding
principles did not get its own and proper place.

Most of the time there are several guiding principles active in an organisation. This certainly is the case in bigger, more complex, organisations
that resulted from mergers or takeovers. Often you can see that parts of
such organisations prefer one of the guiding principles, resulting in conflicts between parts of the organisation, arising out of their loyalty to different principles. An example: in an academic hospital there are at least
three guiding principles: training, research and patient care. The tension
between training and care was once expressed as: *"How many deaths do*
we accept in order to train a doctor?"

If, on the shop floor for example, a discussion arises about what exactly
is the most important thing to be, then it is helpful if the leadership clarifies
that and – in case there is more than one guiding principle – which comes
first. Sometimes you can, eventually, feel the tension at the functional
level. A common function, in many public transport companies, is that of
service and safety. Does safety have priority over service or is it the other
way round? And what happens when a member of staff decides this for
himself? And what is its effect on recruitment and selection? Do people
need to have a friendly and open attitude, or be authoritarian. A company
that wants to provide friendly, safe and cheap transport needs to clarify
which comes first, second and third.

Questions to explore the origin

- Who were the founders? What place do they have?
- Who took the initiative?
- What was the desire, the ideal and the inspiration?
- What was the original guiding principle?

- Who else made it possible that they started?
- What was the launch date?
- Who was the first to give the organisation some traction?
- Who were the first customers?
- What were the first products?
- Where did the first funding come from?
- What was the first structure of the organisation?
- What was the cost of starting? And who paid it?

3.5 History

Acknowledgement of the history constitutes the basis for the present.

> **"** *If you do not know your history, you have no future.* **"**
>
> *Herman Tjeenk Willink:*
> *Vice-President of the Council of State of the Netherlands*

- The door to the future opens via the past
- Remarkable events
- Acknowledgement of what came before
- Questions to explore the history

The door to the future opens via the past

> **"** *The past is not behind us, as we may think, but in front of us. The shadow of what was, casts itself before us: what died is still existing and precedes us.* **"**
>
> *Henry Bataille: French dramatist and poet, 1872-1922*

Much has happened since the start-up. Whatever occurred since then has helped make the organisation what it is now. Without the history, the coming and going of people, teams, products and target groups, the current organisation would be different.

It empowers the system when the contributions of everyone and everything are seen; then the past can be quietly supportive instead of clamouring for attention.

Do you know those foyers where the door before you will not open until the door behind you has closed itself? A clever solution that ensures the occupants don't constantly sit in a draft. Not so convenient, however, for an unsuspecting visitor who wants to enter quickly. Before noticing the system you run into the door that is still closed. As they are usually made of glass you are looking at where you want to go; visually you are already inside.

Organisational change is like being in such a foyer. You cannot start with the new before really finishing what is behind you. The door to the future opens only when the door to the past has closed itself. If you think you can slam closed the door to the past, then you are making a mistake. The past wants to be seen and given its true value. One way or another, it works with this and any other fundamental systemic need, ensuring that they continue to make themselves known until they get the attention they require.

"We're done with bringing up old issues again and again!" is often the wish of the change agent. He wants to go forward. But, apparently, there – in the old story – is something essential that has not been heard and recognised (or not enough). The desire of old stories usually is just to be certain the message in the story is understood. Once that has happened the story can reabsorb itself into the history.

This does not mean that everything has to stay as it is. If the past gets its place and honour, it really opens up the possibility to go forward. Then the past gives strength and foundation to the present, so that everyone and everything can focus on the future.

Remarkable events

The organisation, as a system, requires awareness of its history. This does not mean that all the people who worked for a company during the last hundred years need to be seen and honoured individually. Neither does it imply that all changes in departments and functions should be remembered forever. As with any other living system there are events that have a connection with the essence of the organisation, major events that were the stepping stones to the present.

Switching to a project-based organisation, for example, has an effect on where people belong and also on the ordering of places in the organisation. So we can see that at least two of the five fundamental needs are involved. This certainly makes the switch a significant event. People might remember it; perhaps in terms of 'before' and 'after'. There are usually a number of key events. *"Did this happen before or after the new director? Was it before or after the merger, the division, that accident, that event?"*

They are the kinds of events that taught something to the organisation as a living organism. They are anchored in its memory.

We do not call each other to account!

There is this department that works to this code: "We do not call each other to account." However, everyone feels and says it is impractical not to do so. And so, people address each other indirectly, via so-called jokes or by gossiping. Looking back now, the cause can be attributed to a remarkable event in this department: once there was a meeting of the whole group, where everyone blurted-out everything they thought or felt about their colleagues in the group. This irreparably damaged long-standing friendships: some colleagues went on sick leave and one colleague asked to be transferred. Although only one or two of the present staff had taken part in that session, the past, unconsciously, was playing its role. The helping intervention here, is to look back at that meeting and acknowledge the fact that it came with a high cost.

If the unconscious past is brought into consciousness, it can even reinforce the present. This department has started giving positive feedback to each other and will – through learning from the past – provide further feedback only if people ask for it and, preferably, in a dialogue. Later on, the team will look for a good next step to strengthen cooperation and promote professional behaviour.

The merger

There are two major expertise centres. The authorities see it as logical that a small part of one centre becomes a part of the other centre. Explaining this to the people involved seems to be easy and to go well – perhaps because they are scientists, involved, mainly, in their own specialities; rational people who think analytically. Eventually, about fifteen people move from one centre to the other, which is located in a different town.

Not everything moves with them: they leave their old colleagues, old tasks, the old building and a whole history behind. The new manager decides that the first work-meeting in the new structure will be held at the old building. Perhaps only because the new-location colleagues are in the old workplace, they show attention and develop an understanding of their old-location colleagues' background. Their new workmates proudly show them their old workplace; the tools and equipment they left behind, the colleagues who remained. In passing, they tell them about their pride in the roots of their former institution. After the work meeting they feel seen, not only in who they are as people and staff, but also their background. They were able to show what they took with them and what they left behind. This opened the space, in turn, for them to become interested in the origin of the new centre to which they now belong. In this way, the background of the newcomers can be seen and respected, allowing it to give support without always calling for attention through phrases such as: "But, at our old place this (or that) was much better."

SIEBKE KAAT AND ANTON DE KROON

Acknowledgement of what came before

Not only the origin and remarkable events belong to the system. Everyone who has contributed should be seen as belonging to the system. The new CEO, who expresses her appreciation for the contributions to the company of the technical support services manager with his 28 years service, and of the doorkeeper with his two years service, gives recognition to what was there before. Even though she is much higher in the hierarchy, on the day of her entry into the company she has the least length of service. She must realise that, in this respect, she is the younger one, and at the same time, as the boss, simply do her job.

If any new leader starts by explaining his vision about the, in his eyes, much-needed changes, systemically-speaking he makes a false start.Even though he has been appointed exactly because of his vision of the nature and direction of change needed, he does the necessary justice to the whole by mentioning appropriately and correctly the importance of what has been performed so far.

Subsequently, he can also say, clearly and respectfully, that this does not mean that, in the future, everything can stay as it is. Painful measures, such as the dismissal of people, the elimination of departments or the sale of assets might occur. The system, and the people within it, sense infallibly whether they receive real recognition or not, whether they are just laid off or honestly thanked for their contribution.

Questions to explore the history

- Were there key events, structural changes, dismissals?
- Were goals, products, departments or functions dismissed?
- Were new goals, products, branches added?
- Did the first customers stay? Were new markets entered?
- What happened to the first customers?
- Were there products/services that were harmful and caused accidents?

- Who left? Was it quietly, or in conflict, or with an appropriate farewell?
- Were there flows of money that dried up? Were new ones added?
- What was lost due to lack of care?
- Was injustice done in the past? Where? To whom?
- Who or what is insufficiently seen and honoured?
- What keeps returning?

3.6 Belonging

The thirteenth fairy

Once upon a time, in a faraway country, lived a king and a queen who were very eager to have a baby. Many years passed and, eventually, a beautiful daughter was born. They were so happy! They wanted to celebrate with everyone they knew; all their friends and relatives were invited to a grand feast and also, of course, the fairies of the kingdom.

It was the custom that each fairy would grant a wish. The queen wanted to honour them by serving their food on golden plates. However, she only had twelve golden plates, while there were thirteen fairies. She decided that she would not invite the fairy who lived in the most remote part of the kingdom: it was very likely that the news of the princess's birth would not travel so far.

On the appointed day the great party was held. Each of the fairies, in turn, granted the princess a wish. Each promised her even more beautiful things than the last.

At precisely the moment the eleventh fairy spoke of the great wish she would grant, the thirteenth fairy stormed into the banquet hall. She was furious.

Before anyone could stop her, she flew to the cradle in which the princess lay and said: "On her fifteenth birthday, while working at the spinning wheel, she will injure herself with the shuttle and drop dead!"

SIEBKE KAAT AND ANTON DE KROON

Then she rushed out of the palace, leaving the king, queen and all the guests in shock.

Hesitantly, the twelfth fairy came forward and spoke softly: "I cannot undo the spell cast by another fairy, but I can soften it. The princess will not drop dead, but she will sleep for one hundred years."

And so it came to pass and, to this day, the story of Sleeping Beauty is still told.

Thus, fairies become witches when their existence is ignored. Denying someone the right to belong will, inevitably, manifest in some way.

All that belongs has the right to be a part

> **"** *We share the air with the woods and the water with the seas. As a body, they and we are one.* **"**
>
> **A Tibetan saying**

- Everything that belongs is valued
- Belonging no more
- The switch to a different system
- Questions to explore the belonging

Everything that belongs is valued

The systemic, fundamental need for belonging has to do with facts, not with feelings. You belong to the organisation because, for example, you are on the payroll, even though you might not have a feeling of belonging. It reinforces the organisation when everybody who belongs has a place in the chain of the larger whole; when all the departments, products, as well as the aforementioned origin and history, have their places. Perhaps on the website, in the organisation chart or in some other way.

We are inclined to draw the circle around an organisation rather smaller than bigger: who and what will belong if you make the circle a little wider?

And when you make it even wider? And even more? Who and what comes more clearly into vision then? All those who brought the organisation to where it is today, belong. Every person who reports to a particular manager belongs to his team. All the products or services that the company offers, or has offered in the past, belong to the company. Without customers, no organisation. So the customers belong; including the angry, dissatisfied customers or the ones that left. One can draw ever-wider circles around an organisation.

Looking through systemic glasses you see different subsystems that are interconnected and yet distinct. Each part, every team, each division can be considered as a discrete system. It needs its own function and place, as well as clarity about who belongs and who doesn't. Each subsystem has a beginning, a history and a purpose.

The healthier a subsystem is, the more it is able to open up to, and maintain relationships with, the greater whole to which it belongs, without fear of disintegrating.

Systemically seen, it is interesting to explore where an organisation, or parts of it, spontaneously draw the system's boundaries. Are there groups or elements that, perhaps, are excluded or forgotten? And the question arises whether room has really been made for the new that was added. Or does it remain unconnected?

Where do you belong?

It strengthens both the whole and the part when everything and everyone has a clear place and knows where he primarily belongs. But it is not always that clear...

The store manager

The store manager: to what/where is his primary belonging? Is it to the chain of stores, to the store where he is working, to the group of store managers, or is his strongest bond with his colleagues in 'his' store. Or perhaps with the village where the store is located? And what if every store manager makes his own choice and interpretation?

SIEBKE KAAT AND ANTON DE KROON

Does a judge first of all belong to the profession of judges or to the court where she works?

Does the chip shop belong more to the neighbourhood where the business is established or to the other chip shops in the town? Is that different for coffee shops?

How long does somebody, on long-term sick leave, belong to the department? Does a trainee belong? And the employee who is due to retire? Who have forfeited the right to belong from a moral perspective, but from the systemic perspective still do belong?

Confusion about belonging weakens not only an individual member of staff but the organisation too.

Belonging without having a place

It is strange but true: there are people who have no function but are still on the payroll. They belong to the organisation, but have no place. In some organisations they are called idle bureaucrats. A director complained about such a person. He was not performing at all. He was a nuisance and a gossip. But the director could not discipline him because, as he had no function, there could not be a performance assessment. Naturally, the organisation – as a system - pushes this person to kick up dust, until he has been seen and justice has been done to the principle that everyone who belongs has a clear place. And it is all the more unpleasant when the director says: "I really wanted to give him a clear place but his intolerable behaviour made it impossible." And so, by not saying a proper farewell to one employee, a big energy leak was created affecting the entire organisation.

Belonging no more

If employees, products or projects do not really get a place within the whole – however much they belong – then, ultimately, this invalidates the entire system. This can manifest itself in a sense of insecurity, reduced loyalty or looser ties with the organisation.

These symptoms are ways the organisation, as a system, draws attention to the fundamental need that all who belong are entitled to have a place. And that all who don't belong, or no longer contribute to the system, should leave in an appropriate way.

If you can lose your place or can be fired without warning, how can those that remain still connect themselves without holding back to some degree?

On the other hand, it is also interesting to see who claims a place that is not, or no longer, there for him and what this might tell us systemically. Take, for example, the retired person who frequently drops by his old place of work, or the former employee who constantly 'forgets' to hand in his company ID. Did the organisation really thank them, or is something still needed before the people concerned and the organisation can let go of each other?

Maybe you have even experienced it yourself: when it becomes clear that you are going to apply for another job, in effect you have already left your place and do not belong anymore. When it becomes clear that a department will be sold, then it is already gone. And then comes the crucial question. Is the department dumped in the garbage, or is it given a fitting send-off?

Two philosophical questions. Is it ever possible to separate from a system? Is it really possible to stop belonging?

It is striking how, at the beginning of a training course, people are happy and willing to talk about where they started their careers; at which company. And also, how important it is for them to say in which places and functions, in that company, they were employed. Apparently, all of this belongs with who you are.

Public transport contracts

Dutch public transport is organised via public contracts. As a result of a public tender, a transport company emerges that earns the exclusive, but temporary, right to supply public transport within a certain region.

What does it mean for the bus drivers who are to be transferred – together with the bus routes – to another company? What does it mean

---

SIEBKE KAAT AND ANTON DE KROON

for the element of belonging to the new company, knowing that, after the next public contract, they could well belong to yet another different company? Where do they belong more: to their bus route, to the region they serve, to the company, to the public transport sector? What does it mean to be the driver of a different bus, to wear a new uniform, to comply with new rules and procedures? What does it mean to the manager who is now in charge of a group of drivers and an area, but temporarily? What is the effect on the company that it consists of several concessions, which all expire at different times? Here the key word is acknowledgement. It is as it is: the bond, the belonging here is a temporary one. It is not so strange that people connect less. Being the new employer or the new manager and recognising this, could open a new way to an appropriate commitment.

And how do you say goodbye to those who have to leave the company due to the new contract. People that might have been working there for many years? Sometimes the 'old faithful' receive a send-off in the form of a double row of colleagues to the exit. A beautiful, old ritual in which recognition is given without words, opening the way to go, and to let go, honourably. A different question is whether it is appropriate to allow the newcomers to enter via the same double row.

Where, in fact, do you belong?

It looks like an easy question. But still ... In a matrix organisation, there is this permanent struggle. Do I belong to the region, with the regional manager as my immediate boss, or do I belong to the colleagues in my profession, with the technical program manager as my functional boss? And should every single employee decide this for himself or does the organisation have rules to help you understand this? Conflicts about loyalties, and struggles for power, are being offered – like drinks on a tray – where each individual has to choose for himself, because there is no 'official' recognition of the tension around belonging to two systems.

And what about the senior member of staff? A post that often is created to relieve the manager. The senior member frequently takes care of the planning and the scheduling. But, if he also has a role in performance interviews, does he then still belong to the group of colleagues, or does he belong to the management, or is he without a place, as he actually belongs to none of them? You can, then, expect certain symptoms to show, because self-regulation will always cut-in when someone does not get their real place. As a systemic phenomenon, the senior member could try to prove that he can do better than the manager (having his eye on becoming a manager and so belonging to management), or does he keep team matters under his hat (making it clear that he belongs to the team), or is he positioning himself as a content expert (showing he has his own place, separate from both the team and the management)?

The switch to a different system

A characteristic of organisational systems is that you can join them and can leave them. Moreover, within the system, one can change places.

The soft or the hard approach?

A role in the organisation is eliminated, making the person in the post superfluous. You can imagine several scenarios:

If necessary, someone diligently works to create a new place for this person. Everything is focussed on searching for a new place. And when a new place is finally found, the person involved has no choice but to be grateful and to accept it. However, the mourning, for the loss of the previous function, often remains strong.

Or, attention is paid to what the person contributed while in his function. And it is true that good reasons exist for this place to be removed now. On the one hand, he is being thanked accordingly. On the other hand, to him and others, it is clear that, from now on, he no longer has a place. Only then does the parting become a fact. Both the employee and the organisation are now separated from each other.

Perhaps there are still opportunities, perhaps not. If he will be selected again it is because of who he is: his qualities, capacities, his motivation for a new place and the degree to which he wants to commit himself.

What gives the most strength and dignity to the person? What strengthens the organisation most? What is most appropriate for the colleagues? Which intervention strengthens the manager, the person involved and the team?

Where do or did you belong?

A curriculum vitae helps you to enter somewhere, to present yourself to a system to which you would like to belong. One of the things the people of the new system will need is an understanding of how you connected with previous systems. Are you someone who easily hops from one organisation to another? How did you leave the last one? Why? If someone speaks positively about the last place where he belonged, what effect does it have on you? And what if someone speaks negatively about it? Who are you more inclined to want, to let in?

It is increasingly expected that you bring into your new organisation your existing network of contacts and connections, built up in other companies. And what about the private systems with which we are becoming familiar through social media? The boundaries between private, public and work systems seem to be less and less clear. What does this mean for bonding in a new system?

Starting again with a clean slate is no longer possible. But what if your old slate is not clean enough? Will you then forfeit the possibility to ever access important networks of systems? And if so, what could be your reaction? With whom do you then connect?

Questions to explore the belonging

- Which departments, products, functions, branches and customers belong?
- Which parts are easily forgotten?
- Do these belong: the temporary workers, trainees, flex- and freelance workers, part-timers, the chronically ill, colleagues on temporary transfers and so on?

- Who are the people that are specially, or not at all, invited to 'commitment' rituals, such as annual retreats, social events, or the New Year's Party?

- Who, de facto, do not belong, but still get a place? That one staff member who is in the management team, or the external consultant who takes part in a team outing, or the HR colleague who is invited to the department's Christmas Party?

- For which functions is it difficult to say where they belong? Perhaps those that seem to belong everywhere a little bit?

3.7 Order

In the order of the whole, each part has its own place

Praising someone to the sky means denying him his place on earth

---

- Place and order
- Questions to explore the order

Place and order

Any living system, in which the individuals must cooperate in order to survive, cannot exist without order. A pack of wolves, dogs or deer, but also a company, team or association, needs a clear order in which everyone has a distinct place from where he makes his own contribution to the survival of the whole.

Hierarchy is the main ordering principle in a business, visibly depicted in the organisation chart.

This hierarchy is, unlike those of animals, rationally designed to clarify the order and prevent uncertainty or endless attempts to confirm it. The highest in rank determines a company's structure and the conditions within which the others do their work, and this gives him the highest position. The higher a function is placed in the structure, the more important it is for the whole. Of course there is no factory without workers, but they cannot even start working without someone controlling the income, however many workers are available. And without people to manage the factories, machines, licences and work schedules everything would go wrong. In short, those higher in rank and position are there to enable the work, so that the whole can function. The hierarchy is also expressed in salary and benefits. It does not mean that one person – as a human being – is more important or of more value than another!

In addition to hierarchy there are other ordering principles within organisations: the number of years working in a function, seniority within the company, age, skills and so on. Which ordering principles come into play, and in which sequence they are arranged to determine the right order, is different for each organisation. In a general sense one can say that those functions which come first make it possible for others to do their jobs. Most of the time this parallels the hierarchy nicely. And the person who has contributed to the organisation over a longer period, earns a higher place in the order, above those who came later. He is 'entitled to speak' as, through experience, he knows a lot of the history.

Equality between people is a fact, but not all have the same position. Many people are allergic to differences in position. But systemically-seen it brings peace and strength to the system, when each one takes his own place and allows every other person his or hers. Apparent similarity or confusion, about the order, creates disorder. It leads to a struggle around who takes which place, creating a pecking order.

Order is about the way in which all the parts of the system are connected to each other. Everything in its proper place. Every living system has an order, which depends on the contribution of each part to the survival of the whole.

The instructions in the plane are clear: "Parents; first put on your own oxygen mask, only then attend to your child's."

The heart, lungs and brain take precedence over skin and muscles when loss of blood occurs in a human body. In the sharing of food, adult lions get priority over the cubs. The government and the king have a special shelter in case of emergencies and, compared to others, non-managerial departments are more easily outsourced.

Therefore, on an organisation chart, not only the functions are depicted in their mutual relationships, but also the units, departments and teams. There, too, it is the rule, that every part must have its own clear and proper place in the order of the whole.

And, earlier on, we talked about the peace that exists as a result of a clear order of guiding principles.

Looking for young talent

Many companies have programs for young talent, aimed at attracting young, highly-educated professionals. They receive training and the opportunity to find their bearings in the company. They often have several management positions during a short period of time, in order to gain experience in management and to get to know the company in all its facets. Sometimes they do not get a permanent contract, allowing both company and employee to see and experience how things are. Beautiful. The question is, are you only allowed to enrol yourself in this program if you are young and come from outside the company. What effect does this have on talented employees who have the misfortune to already be in the company and happen to be only thirty years of age? What is the effect of this (expensive) program on people who have worked there already for many years, and who would love to get the opportunity to develop themselves via training courses and new work experience, but who are told there is no money for such a program? In other words, what happens if, in the ordering, 'education' is placed above 'experience'? If young comes before middle-aged and old? If not-

---

SIEBKE KAAT AND ANTON DE KROON

connecting is placed above committing yourself, long term, to the company or function?

Systemically seen, you can sit back and wait for the system's self-regulation to restore the right order: an order that does justice to those who brought the system to where it is now. You can wait for the experienced, middle-aged and older colleagues, having connected themselves, heart and soul, for years, to turn against the newcomers ... no matter how much they can see that the new people bring a refreshing new look and approach! The system will also respond in order to do justice to those who have contributed for a long time. For example, by offering existing employees other types of training and the possibility to explore new paths and to move on in their jobs.

Disturbances of the order?

The illustrations below show how order is clarified. If you put yourself in the position of all those involved, as well as in the whole of the organisation, what does it tell you about what is appropriate and what is inappropriate? What reinforces and what weakens the whole?

- The long-term employee who is passed over for promotion, without it being discussed with her.
- The colleague being used by the manager as a buddy and taken into confidence.
- The newcomer who immediately gets his own room, while older colleagues don't have that privilege.
- The part-timer who gets the much-wanted and popular projects and, therefore, does not have to do 'ordinary' work.
- The colleagues, with children, who receive priority to be off work during the school holidays.
- The member of the works council who, in advance of her manager, receives information regarding his department.
- The director; cutting everyone's budgets except his own.
- The older employee receiving privileges that are no longer appropriate.

Questions to explore the order

- Who bear the greatest responsibility for the whole?
- Who have been longer in the company?
- Who have been longest in the department?
- What is the order of the different functions in the organisation?
- What is the hierarchy between direct and indirect personnel?
- In a family business, what comes first: the family or the company?
- What gives additional status or position? Seniority? Age? Place of residence? Education? Expertise? Relationships?
- Does sex, religion, marital status, cultural background or sexual orientation affect one's position? How? What might that say about the origin and history of the organisation?

3.8 Balance

There must be a fair balance between taking and giving

People that give too much overwhelm other people. By doing so, they make it difficult for others to keep the relationship in balance.

People that take too much exhaust the relationship.

- Balance between taking and giving
- A special contribution
- Questions to explore the balance

Balance between taking and giving

The balance between taking and giving is concerned with the exchange that takes place between parts of the system: between management layers, between staff and management, between departments, between colleagues, between the organisation and its employees. This exchange also deals with the balance of taking and giving between the organisation and its clients, customers, and investors. Exchange also takes place between the organisation and its physical environment. Does it exhaust the earth by mining raw materials? Does it damage the area? Where the balance is fair, all parties (systems) involved become stronger. Where the balance is unequal, one part exhausts the other by taking too much or giving too little. A system which is maintained in a state of imbalance – for example by not honouring some aspects from the past, or by uncertainty about who belongs to the system and who has which place – can easily be diagnosed via a disturbance in the balance of taking and giving. The symptoms that can appear are staff turnover (no longer wanting to invest your own energy), absenteeism (no longer being able to invest), failing to do what has been agreed (by belonging more to something else), income dropping and so on.

If the balance between taking and giving is in a state of equilibrium, this manifests as freedom between parties. The freedom to go, the freedom to stay. There is no mortgage by the past on the future. Accordingly, everyone can deploy his full energy; any new movement can start freely.

Sometimes one part of the system gives so much to another part that it is impossible for the receiver to endure taking it. To keep one's sense of dignity there is no other solution than to end the relationship.

The failure of the relationship

An assistant to the team leader is always doing too much. He almost takes over his boss's function. The team leader seems unable to restrict his assistant, who explains that he loves the work he does. Both the relationship and the order are becoming distorted. The more the assistant is taking over without being asked, the more irritable the team leader becomes and the more distance he puts between the assistant and himself, literally and figuratively. When he needs extra help he now prefers to ask others, making the assistant feel even more overlooked and undervalued: after all, isn't he the one who is investing so much! In the end the team leader feels he has no choice but to ask the HR department to find a new place for the assistant, out of the team. His investment and commitment surely require recognition, a reward, 'something' in return.

But when someone gives such a large amount, nothing is big enough to balance it. Moreover it feels inappropriate, as the assistant gave far too much without being asked. For his colleagues, his being compensated – in whatever form – would send the message: "Doing your work very well is not good enough." *With the result that people might stop investing their energy (because it will never be enough) and others might find themselves, unconsciously, trying to follow the example of the assistant. In this way the imbalance between the assistant and the team leader becomes an imbalance that invalidates the whole system. When the assistant has been reallocated he is still filled with incomprehension and resentment. His former colleagues and team leader breathe a collective sigh of relief.*

The team leader has learned his lesson: he will offer a coach to the next person who does excessive overtime; to find out where the pattern of limitless investing originates and how he can handle it, in a constructive way, for himself and for the whole.

A special contribution

From way back, companies have given employees special rewards: the bigger the organisation, the more the criteria for the award have been considered and perfected. The same applies to length-of-service awards. The recipients have earned a special place for themselves.

Systemically, it works the same way. Departments or people, that have contributed in a special way, deserve acknowledgement for that. Not forever, but in a way that is appropriate. The contribution could be commemorated in a management-team meeting, during a new year's speech, or in an annual report.

Sometimes a commemorative plaque is right. Just think of the many places where war dead are commemorated. They contributed by giving their lives.

An example: the youngest trainee, who discovers a potential fire risk and takes appropriate action, did something special for the survival of the company. He ends up on the front page of the staff journal and, perhaps, he gets a special gift.

In the event that a special contribution is not acknowledged, the system itself begins to look for a way to draw attention to this.

Acknowledgement of a special contribution has a limit. If the giver and receiver of the special recognition fail to return to normal – which means to be in the right relationship, the right order – then one becomes the prisoner of the other. The debt of never being able to give or get enough arises.

A special award, to acknowledge a special contribution, makes the whole organisation viable if everyone involved is able to continue in the proper relationship and order. Too many people have been kicked upstairs.

How can I ever thank you enough?

An entrepreneur, the maker of a very special product, is being accused of violating patents. He is absolutely convinced he has done nothing of the kind. But the other party starts legal action … and you never know how a judge will rule.

All the employees of his company, as well as some supporters (customers, lawyers, investors) are committed to helping him and the company.

The lawsuit is won, joy abounds, bankruptcy averted. The entrepreneur feels extremely grateful. "Without this huge extra effort we wouldn't have made it." He seeks advice about how to show his gratitude, in a good way, to all who helped. The employees have already received flowers, cake and champagne. They have their particular relationship with the company: delivering extra effort was directly in their own interest. Bankruptcy would have meant the end of their jobs. That balance has been restored.

Talking to the consultant, something important becomes clear to the entrepreneur; all of the external helpers have their own unique relationship with him. Their contribution was an investment in their relationship with …? Yes, with whom or what actually? With him in person? With the company? With the product? With …?

When he starts to consider the extent of the possible relationships he gives up on the idea of doing something for all the external helpers combined.

Subsequently, he struggles with the answer to this question. "How can I thank those people for their incredibly-large contribution? What would be a suitable expression of my enormous gratitude?" *What is appropriate recognition when someone gives you a really large gift? One for which you cannot compensate by giving back an equally large gift? If such giving back is not an option, how would it be to acknowledge it like this:* "Thank you for all you gave me, knowing that I could never return it in kind." *Is this eternal gratitude? How does this affect the relationship? How is it, to be in someone's debt forever? How is it for the other person, knowing that, whatever he receives, he will always be entitled to more? Can you feel the alienation this causes?*

For the consultant, this is the reason to find out whether the entrepreneur has any idea of the phenomenon of appropriate gratitude – or that he, more or less, can feel what it is. The consultant then asks: "What did you do when you were little and your parents gave you a toy you really wanted?" *The entrepreneur answers:* "I showed my gratitude by getting totally absorbed in my present and having lots of fun." *A few moments later the entrepreneur says:* "Now I know."

He had discovered this beautiful way of passing on his thankfulness, through his own actions, as an ultimate acknowledgement of the gift he had received.

Questions to explore the balance

- Is there a place where the exchange between taking and giving comes to a standstill: in the organisation, in the relationship with its customers or suppliers?

- Does a fair balance exist between accountability and power, payment and position?

- Is attention being given to people celebrating their length-of-service?

- How does the organisation bid farewell to employees?

- Does everyone get equal training opportunities? Do the differences, if any, appear fair?

- Is there a lot of absenteeism, staff turnover, burnout?

- How are the salaries, compared to other businesses in the same market? Are they in balance? What effect does this have on the relationship between individual employees and the company?

- Is overtime paid?

- How are voluntary services rewarded?

- How are issues of trust handled? Working from home, having a company car and phone?

- Why do employees stay? For the salary, nice colleagues, interesting work, learning opportunities, freedom or something else?

- Is the organisation involved in corporate social responsibility: sustainability activities, in charities, in the environment in which it operates?

3.9 Patterns

- Identification

- Contaminated places

- Unavailable places

- Non-existent places

- Parentification

- Recurring patterns

If, at any time within an organisation, the five fundamental needs are not met, phenomena will appear to bring attention to this situation. When the origin and/or history are being neglected, or when an office-holder has more than one place or none, or when the order is unclear or reversed, or when parts of the system are treated as only half belonging or not at all, then any of these states will produce disturbances that cause symptoms. Also, these states can always be identified by a disruption in the balance of taking and giving. The problem you then see is, systemically, no more than a direction indicator. You must look further than the balance between people or departments; look to the past, to the connection, to the order. The art of the practice comes in recognising what is being made visible as a systemic signal and not just to dismiss it as the individual problem of a random worker.

If one or more of the fundamental needs are being neglected, the system reacts to this violation of its vitality. It will continue to react as long as nothing happens to meet those ignored needs. Let's take a short trip to another living system. When the lead elephant dies, fighting occurs in the herd for as long as is necessary to establish a new order, or until it has become clear that this group can no longer be a single herd. Then it splits into two herds, each with its own order. The struggle for power arises, between various parts of the system, to clarify who belongs and, subsequently, everyone's place in the order.

There are patterns that frequently show themselves in organisations. Usually they have to do with order: people who do not, or are not able, to take the place that goes with their function – due to something from the past, related to that place, which is still being neglected. These patterns probably occur so often in organisations, because the people operate in multiple systems. It can happen that they carry a pattern over from one system to another. (This will be covered, in more detail, in Chapter Five: Systemic Coaching). Moreover, organisations are so complex, with frequently-changing structures (orders), functions and extra hats (double positions), that it is easy to see why confusion occurs easily in the domains of belonging and order. The past also lays in wait for those who do not take it into account when replacing personnel (too) quickly. Now we will look into some frequently-repeating patterns that originate from insufficient honouring of one or more of the fundamental systemic needs, described earlier.

Identification

This pattern can arise if there is a threat that something essential to the organisation might be lost. Some way or other, people, functional groups or even complete departments identify with a guiding principle, a goal or an ambition that, suddenly and unexpectedly, threatens to fall out of the picture. Behind this manifestation, however, is a strong bond with something that is crucial to the vitality of the organisation.

Acknowledgement of skills

The company had grown because it put craftsmanship first. From the beginning, it was a technically-oriented, male-dominated business. The person with the most subject-matter expertise would become a manager. Colleagues easily accepted the lack of 'people skills' as this was compensated by expert knowledge and a broad insight into all the stages of the company's development. These are the kind of people who know how to get things done, who are familiar with the background of failure-as-learning and share their passion for craftsmanship with their colleagues.

Then the change came. From outside, highly-educated and well-trained managers were brought in to the company. Many were young and inexperienced: qualified industrial engineers or graduates in social sciences. All of a sudden female managers appeared. People really liked them and, yes, they were very good at the art of conversation. They empathised, saw employees as human beings. But still …? Increasingly, people identified themselves with their technical craftsmanship and jargon began to reappear.

A systemic reflection. What was the signal for them to start behaving in these ways? Did they use jargon to exclude the new managers? Or to include the technical background, without which the company could not have become what it is now? Or to honour their former managers? If you were to ask them, they would look at you strangely, in surprise. Because it wasn't them making a conscious choice, it was the system reacting.

And of course they made use of the old managers – now known as 'experts' – to get things done in the organisation. In this way, an informal organisational structure started, which became stronger than the formal one, and caused an endless flow of new managers in and out of the company. It lasted until the board decided that the new leadership structure did not work, in spite of underlying good intentions. A deep understanding of employees' functions became a key requirement for new managers.

Contaminated places

Particularly from your 'outsider' position, you can often see very clearly that people, occupying certain posts, are leaving significantly faster than would be normal in such an organisation. Somehow they cannot put down roots. And it is in the roots or, to put it another way, in the past, that the cause of this phenomenon lies. Did a predecessor leave in a systemically-strange way? Did terrible, strange or unmentionable things happen? Was this predecessor really thanked enough for his contribution? Even if he had to leave due to misconduct?

The systemic, fundamental need of belonging only lets someone go – making the place really free to be occupied by someone else – when the end-balance of taking and giving is fair, in which justice is done to the fact that the person belonged. Has everything been given its due? Have all profits, guilt and pain been really accepted? Have acknowledgement and thanks been given?

Wherever something necessary is lacking, the system will generate a symptom for it, asking for attention to this energy leak in the system. Due to the fact that people are continuously leaving a particular position, the system sends out a powerful message: you must deal respectfully with all who once belonged, otherwise you will never be able to give new people the feeling that they really belong. Only when acknowledgement has been made, of the person with whom the turnover began (and this can easily be done by saying it in a management meeting), can his successors, who couldn't stay either, also be acknowledged. In this way the place can be made clear and free for the person who is there now, and the pattern of not wanting, or being able to belong, can be released.

It's just not working out for me here!

A director wanted coaching, for one of his managers whom his colleagues didn't trust. The manager was quite new at this place and had an impressive CV. That is why the conflict was so confronting, both for the director and the manager. The director began to doubt the manager's ability and offered him coaching. When, during their first meeting, the coach asked the director if anything had happened with the function the new manager had taken, it became silent. "How long have you got?" said the director. A picture emerged of managers who, for various reasons, only stayed a short while in this function.

Suddenly, it struck the director that maybe this phenomenon could mean something other than that the managers didn't 'fit' in some way. He remembered, very well, the person with whom this pattern of premature leaving began. It had never been clear why this manager had to leave. Everyone assumed it had something to do with fraud, but no one really knew and it was never made official. This person had left quietly, without a goodbye.

What effect does it have on your trust of the management if your boss commits fraud? If your boss leaves without a farewell? When his managers say nothing about his leaving, when they hush up the other people involved? It isn't strange that distrust arises where existing trust was severed abruptly. Via this conversation, interventions arose that were different to those that could have been thought of beforehand. The question about the director and the manager developed into: How can we acknowledge the history – with all its loose ends?

Unavailable places

It also happens that a place is, actually, not available – not in fact, but systemically – because it is still occupied by a predecessor. It is as if the previous person still occupies the place in such a way that, somehow, it cannot be taken. The new member of staff learns this by experiencing difficulty in applying his normal qualities and talents. He cannot find his courage, authority, initiative: qualities that were readily available in previous roles. It is exactly this observation that makes it worthwhile to look at the history of this place, this role. This pattern often is related to the fact that the predecessor did not properly leave the post. Often, when people move internally, the organisation fails to give explicit recognition to what that person achieved and contributed in their previous role. But it is just as necessary 'internally'.

On the one hand to let him go well; on the other hand to make the place available for his successor. Sometimes a person does move to another place, but appears to be occupying his former place at the same time. Apparently, a system needs to say farewell to someone who had a place in the system, in order to free that place systemically. This can completely release the outgoing employee from his old function and allow him to dedicate all his energy and attention to his new role, without any sense of guilt. The system will always make this pattern clear: colleagues might approach the previous person as if he was still in his old function, or just might not give the new person a chance.

Non-existent places

In addition to the contaminated and unavailable places there is another variation: the non-existent place. A place without a raison d'être in the organisational system; a place artificially invented and created. You can recognise when someone is in such a place by the way colleagues always seem to 'forget' him (in his function!). At an individual level he is able to get things done, but his function seems to have no weight at all. And, in reality, this is true: systemically it doesn't exist. Because there is no reason for it to do so, or it's raison d'être is no longer valid. This phenomenon is known to all supernumerary staff, to all who are outsourced in the short or long run, or the ones whose places are created in order to give them a job, where no job actually exists. You are there and not there at the same time, or there less and less, or always a little bit there. The painful element is that these constructions always are created to offer something to the person concerned: time to find another job, the possibility of still belonging and so on. The effect is that employees experience it as either not belonging or belonging less and discover that they cannot contribute any longer. Before you know it they are blaming themselves, damaging their self confidence and, with it, their chances of finding another job. The system makes the following clear: when a function or department is no longer important to the survival of the system then, literally, there is no longer a place for it. Sometimes a person needs to fail persistently at a certain post before the decision is taken to abolish that position (due to it being superfluous). The reverse can happen too. People then take the removal of a place personally, as if it is not the place but they who must be blamed for the failure. In this way a personal drama and a positive systemic effect can end up in conflict with each other; maybe with a high price being paid by both sides.

SIEBKE KAAT AND ANTON DE KROON

Please stay!

Before he took office the new director had already heard there were many staff problems in the department. So he created the function of HR manager. He was happy with the person appointed, a well-experienced HR professional. The chosen person was also very happy: a good chance to move into management.

As time went by, this manager felt increasingly drained and ineffective, yet had no idea why. He felt valued within the management team and the team leaders were satisfied with him: "He makes smart observations and has very good ideas. He's always prepared to make time for you and he is well informed; a nice, capable and interested person." And yet he felt his vitality was being undermined.

What had not changed, with the creation of the new function, was that all the staff issues remained to be the responsibility of the team leader concerned. And there also was an HR consultant available, to be consulted in all personnel matters.

Indeed, a place was created, but the relationship and interaction with the other parts of the organisation was missing. Whatever the HR manager did, he always had to take someone else's place to do it: that of the team leader, the HR consultant or the director. This made it clear that the organisation did not have a proper place for him. When, in such a case, a person does his very best to be successful and to create his own place, then it costs the individual concerned a great deal, while bringing nothing that could not have been achieved in a different way. A side effect of creating your own, informal, place is that it is extremely difficult to leave that situation: you cannot handover a non-existent place, as it exists merely by the grace of you as a person and the network you built up yourself. Leaving feels like letting yourself down and having worked for nothing.

Parentification

This concept originates from Minuchin, a family therapist. Parentification is the pattern in which the child takes the position of the parents. In the context of an organisation it means the pattern of someone adopting an inner attitude of being above the leadership. This attitude is: *"I know better than my boss"* or *"In fact, I should have been the director here; I can do his job better than him."* In this way the parentified person undermines the position of his leader, and that of the leader's leader too.

The senior leader should, after all, do something about this failing leadership, shouldn't he? So the employee is vacating his own place, because he judges himself too big for it. In short, parentification is a serious signal that the order is asking for attention. A system is strongest when everyone takes his own place. A function works best if the person who has accepted that function takes only the place that goes with it. In cases of parentification, people take other places, vacating their own, which has a negative effect on both the parts and the whole. Parentification is the system making an emergency intervention. The place that has not been taken by, for example, the leader becomes a vacuum sucking at the system. Someone stepping in temporarily creates some rest. But, due to this relatively restful result, management is unlikely to intervene. So you can see that, sometimes, things must get worse – perhaps team members falling ill, or harassing each other, or underperforming – before senior management puts pressure on the formal leader. This is a kind of self-regulation: the order is determined anew. We see the pattern of parentification functioning as both signal and repair. In a healthy system, when the signal becomes powerful enough, self-regulation arises and parentification is no longer needed.

Sometimes, intervention by higher management clarifies that the original qualifications, needed for a particular managerial position, are no longer appropriate or good enough. Then the system needs to be organised in a different way. Sometimes it becomes clear that the personality of the manager makes him unsuitable for the role. This means he must leave. Sometimes it is the parentified person who pays a price. (Often we see this in the way whistle-blowers are treated). Most of the time he is put back into the team without any thanks or honour because, from the point of view of the management, no putting back is needed: after all, he was just a member of the team all the time, wasn't he? Claiming a different place, in an informal way, does not bring thanks and honour for doing so. The person who informally steps out of his own subsystem – the team – violates the belonging, so much, that usually there is no longer a place for him in his 'own' team. And so it happens that, for these people, there is no longer a place available anywhere in the system.

There are several variations of leaving one's own place. Sometimes an employee becomes his boss's buddy, or the leader chooses a team member to 'lean' on. By responding, the team member leaves his own place and, in an informal way, he moves into the subsystem of the management and disorder and loss of energy ensue.

Sometimes you see that a leader really wants to belong to the team. He links up too much with the subsystem of the team members, too little with that of the managers.

This also causes confusion: your manager is your colleague and work-mate, but he also must assess you and implement directives. This confusion can create different symptoms: a rift between management and employees, an unsafe feeling within teams, informal lines of communication that become more important than formal ones and so on.

Because it is crucial that a clear and appropriate order is established in a system, symptoms will always pop up whenever there is lack of clarity about the order. In the end, systemic self-regulation will always arise, but very often coming at a high price: team members that get ill or leave, a manager being removed from his position and people, who stayed too long in informal places, losing their right to a place.

Recurring patterns

Leaving your place can be caused by recurrence of a pattern. When it is difficult for a leader to take his place – perhaps because, in his family of origin, he could not or was not allowed to take his rightful place, or when a colleague, as a child in his family of origin, already was the 'saviour' for his father or mother – then parentification, between the manager and the members of a team, easily manifests. In such a case, the phenomenon is particularly concerned with the repeating of patterns originating in the family systems of the people involved. Coaching, to show this clearly, can give a lot of solace. However, sometimes you see that a pattern is manifesting itself at several places in the organisation. This is a powerful signal that something is not completely 'in order'.

Boundary-crossing behaviour or a connecting ritual?

The consultant was being asked to think along with the head of a division. The figures for harassment, discrimination and intimidation amongst colleagues were too high, much too high, and had been so for some time now. The managers involved had received counselling, which attempted to identify to what the 'crossing-borders' behaviour was related. But, eventually, the managers complained that they felt unsafe. If they did not take part in the rat race, by always being reachable by phone, responding to e-mails during the weekends and evenings and taking on far more than was realistic, then they were afraid they would be fired. The consultant, to the divisional head: "You also tolerate and confirm boundary-crossing behaviour." *He pointed out that, in the head's relationship with him, borders were continuously crossed: meetings cancelled at the last-minute, meetings running over schedule or different people attending than had been agreed with the consultant. In these cases, too, what was unspoken was also very clear:*

"We don't expect you to make a fuss; if you did, we really would ask ourselves if you were the right one for us." *This question arose:* "It looks like the same pattern is continuously repeating itself; you belong, but only if you agree to the code of not making your boundaries clear. What could possibly be its function? What is or has been the problem with connecting and belonging in a logical way?"

SIEBKE KAAT AND ANTON DE KROON

The systemic consultant

4

- Introduction
- When to work systemically?
- Attitude
- Applied knowledge
- Course of action
- Systemic exploring

4.1 Introduction

Thoughtful and cautious is the way.

> **"** *It is about letting go of preconceived ideas, of the tendency to judging and holding onto problems; it is the willingness to discover, to explore and to value what is, with focussed attention and full of trust.* **"**
>
> *Chungliang Al Huang and Jerry Lynch: The Tao of Wisdom*

In this chapter we discuss what it entails for the consultant who wants to work systemically. First of all, there is the question of whether the systemic approach is the right one for the issue in question, in that organisation. And, when it is, what this method means for the client as well as the consultant.

We think that, for the consultant, the most important element is the attitude from which he works. We go quite deeply into this issue. Next, we discuss how to apply what we have learned about the fundamental needs of organisation. Finally, we look at how to act from a systemic attitude. So, in this chapter, we answer these two important questions: what do I, as a systemic consultant, do and how do I do it? The chapter ends with a discussion of some common problems in organisations and explains how to find their systemic roots.

4.2 When to work systemically?

If the problems in an organisation are persistent and interventions bring little, or only temporary relief, then it is apparent that the system needs something else, before the parts of the system can regain their strength.

The systemic approach is appropriate in the following circumstances:

- Patterns repeat themselves in time and place and, perhaps, at more places in the organisation.
- The cause of the patterns is unclear.
- Common interventions are of no lasting help, or of no help at all.
- People show good will but still the interventions don't work.
- Energy seems to flow out of the system, also from newcomers.

Like a garden

It is like your garden; normally all goes well if you water and feed your plants. But there are places where nothing works at all. No matter what you do, everything you plant dies or withers. Maybe, under the surface, there's a layer of concrete, poured long ago? Maybe there is poison in the soil? Maybe that big conifer sucks away water and nutrients, takes all the sunlight and makes the soil acidic. In all these cases, adding manure and water will not help anymore; something different is needed. Here it is necessary to look at the bigger picture in order to discover what is going on.

The systemic approach offers the opportunity for fundamental change, because the people in the system gain insight into the bigger whole in which the problem occurs.

Working systemically also requires something from all those involved. It asks for the courage to let go of preconceived ideas about what is going on, and about how it should be solved. In particular, clients who have to report on change projects to higher management and, perhaps also to workers' councils, can find it difficult not to have a blueprint in advance. Working systemically demands a great deal of trust from all concerned.

First, trust that the system will reveal all the knowledge and information necessary about what is going on and what is needed to effect and sustain change. Then, trust that the members of the system – with the help of an outsider who is able to look and listen with an open-mind and without prejudice – will be able to translate this information into action. And, finally, trust that change can occur without predetermined, precisely-defined steps and deadlines. It also requires a desire to explore what really is the matter. There's no bullshit and the consultant does not take the difficult decisions away from the people appointed to make them.

Moreover, when the client has an exact preconception of what the outcome of an intervention should be – for example reducing the number of people on sick leave by a specific percentage – you cannot work systemically. The same applies to a tight time schedule that determines what needs to be done and when.

Of course there is always an 'obvious' cause and a goal. Together, the consultant and the client start exploring why that goal has yet to be reached and what might be the hidden cause of the high numbers on sick leave. And, as they explore together, completely different interventions might then pop up that, at first sight, seem to have no connection at all with the theme of sick leave.

The client always benefits from a certain kind of curiosity and the consultant from a certain amount of freedom to act. What could possibly be the matter here? What could be needed by the system as a whole? Once the client and consultant have contracted for this kind of cooperation, the path becomes free to walk.

4.3 Attitude

Approaching. What a beautiful word. You approach the other, the organisation. The right attitude is crucial to how you do that. How, as a systemic consultant, do you approach the other person, the organisation? You are getting closer, with all your baggage, all your knowledge of living systems and the principles that empower an organisation. And as you get nearer you register all you perceive. Without any judgement. You receive everything entering your awareness just as information from the system.

You approach with deep respect for this living system. All that happens has an underlying motive. This approach results in an attitude of humility, the foundation for systemic working.

This attitude has a number of aspects, that are inextricably interwoven:

- In service of the whole
- Without judgement
- Detached involvement
- Multilateral partiality
- Temporary place
- Restrained action
- Systemic derailing

Now we describe these aspects and give examples of how they can guide the consultants actions.

In service of the whole

As a systemic consultant you look not only at the part ('problem') for which you have been hired, but also at the organisation as a whole. Whatever your point of action might be – an individual person, a team, a department or a division – you are always working in service of the whole, and not, for example, for the shop floor and against the management, or for a local branch and against the head office. You are always looking for a way to empower the whole so that everyone can do their job well. The bigger whole is always there. If a large multinational company is your client, there exist bigger entities of which even such a large organisation is a part. For example the markets in which the company operates, countries where they have offices or factories or countries to which they export.

This means that the most-senior manager isn't necessarily your only client, or that by involving yourself at other levels, you exceed your authority and your contract.

In harmony?

A consultant was invited in by a ministerial department. Earlier, the top-level management had decided that, due to budget cutbacks, external consultants could no longer be hired. So, this 'invitation' was in direct contradiction of that ruling.

The consultant who, knowing this ruling, still takes this job, judges himself to be better-able to decide what is good for the ministry than the people that have been appointed to do so. So this consultant will never be able to work in service of the whole, no matter how good his intentions or advice might seem.

Working in service of the whole is not driven by ethical considerations. It stems from the observation that the whole provides the foundation for the part. The whole is always stronger than the part. Sometimes, within a whole which is in decline – a retail chain perhaps – a single part, just one branch, might still flourish. But just how long can this part keep flourishing within the decaying larger whole? The parts become stronger to the same degree that the whole becomes stronger; not the other way round. Parts get stronger the more they take their own, right places in the whole.

Or by leaving the whole when everything indicates that there is no longer a place for them. This is the reason that, as a consultant, you commit yourself first of all to the whole and only from there to the part.

Without judgement

> **“** *It demands sensibility and courage to see the world just as it is at every moment, without judgement or criticism.* **”**
>
> **Chungliang Al Huang and Jerry Lewis: The Tao of Wisdom**

Looking systemically demands a special state of being, from where you look at what is, in a completely open way, without any judgement at all.

You clear yourself. You put your knowledge, views, judgements and expertise aside and observe this system; its unique patterns, unique background and its raison d'être.

This open attitude carries the possibility that you might become aware of, discover, something of value to the system.

Looking beyond the problem

A boss said to the consultant: "I think you will agree with me that this employee has gone too far and I have no choice but to take serious action?" *Yes ...? the consultant could see the boss's point and, for a moment or two, he sat back in his chair and opened himself to the boss and his judgement, but also to the employee and all the circumstances and causes. After a short while and a deep breath he spoke.*

"I have an easy solution and a hard solution. The easy one: I share your indignation. You are right. Punish him; then we can forget the whole thing. The hard one: look further. What made this employee behave as he did? Or, what was it that seemed to invite him to do so? If he had not done it, would someone else have done it 'for' him? Has this happened before? In this way, you explore the possibility that it is not so much a personal issue, but the system telling you something about itself. If this is the case, you have rather more to do than discipline the employee. Perhaps the right action is to thank him, because, through his behaviour, he is showing that something is happening that diminishes the power of the system."

In a living system there is a constant interplay of interactions among parts of the whole. We look at these, this behaviour, as ways that the system ensures its survival. Judging these is not appropriate. Therefore, this all-embracing and factual way of looking feels safe and supportive to the people involved. Not only is the buck not passed to anyone, the buck does not even exist. There is no good or bad, guilt or innocence. These terms and concepts belong to a non-systemic world; for example, to the judicial. What is ...? is. And not without reason.

This non-judgemental attitude can be quite confronting, for example, when it becomes crystal clear that a pattern continuously repeats itself and the people involved do not have the authority to change it. Confronting too, because it might become clear that there is no place (or no longer) for certain parts (people) of the system, or that they took places that were not theirs.

Confronting, as it might well become clear that the whole system has no right to exist anymore. You certainly should not want to 'help', although your intervention might be experienced as such. What you really want to do is, together with members of the system, bring the underlying patterns to the surface, the underlying truth. Once these are revealed, experience shows that the appropriate people usually know what to do.

Whereas, most of the time, a 'normal' consultant is asked for his opinion, his view and an astute judgement, the systemic consultant makes an extreme effort to have no opinion or judgement at all. The more judgement you have, the more you depart from the systemic attitude, and the less able you are to see why a system evokes behaviour that is felt as difficult, wrong or 'ill'.

Detached involvement

Letting go of judgements is easier when there is a bit of distance. Simply watching seems to invite better perception, bring more within your reach. It invites the question: what on earth could possibly be the function of the behaviour you are witnessing? Moreover, your involvement is essential too: what do you see in the other person, what do you notice about yourself, what thoughts, what feelings pop up involuntarily? Just by opening yourself to this system and getting into real contact with it, relevant information from the system might appear. 'Without judgement' does not degenerate into aloofness or analysis.

How to connect?

It is like standing at a river's edge with one foot on the bank and the other one in the water, testing the strength of the current and the temperature of the water. You do not jump into the river, because then the current would take you, but you also are not only just standing on the side, contemplating which course to take.

SIEBKE KAAT AND ANTON DE KROON

Multilateral partiality

Detached involvement clears the way for you, as a consultant, to take your place with an attitude of multilateral partiality. This concept is different from neutrality or staying apart. It means letting your judgements evaporate and putting yourself completely in the place of each of the parties involved. As soon as, and for as long as, you are judgemental, you cannot connect in a complete and open way with all the parties, all the places and with what wants to be expressed. With your attitude of multilateral partiality you connect yourself, alternately and continuously, with everyone and everything. Often you notice that this brings completely new perspectives and insights. Sometimes, just sharing them with the members of the system is already enough, giving a point of departure for them to look, feel and act differently. It's not important that they are partial; that's, simply, because they are a part.

The multilateral partial consultant

"We wouldn't have any problem at all if the people in Department A just worked harder," says the director. The consultant checks: "The workers in A are to blame for things going wrong?" *The director confirms. To which the consultant reacts:* "Yes, I could see it that way." *And, after a little while:* "And I have another view too. Do you want me to tell you what that is?" "Yes, of course," *says the director. And then the consultant says that she, looking without any judgement at all, only sees a department doing things differently from the others.*

Or, put another way: the other departments do it differently from A. This question arises in her: "How long has this been the case?" *The director mentions a period of reorganisation where, in the end, a new manager came in and the reins were tightened.* "Everything had become too loose."

That elicited two observations from the consultant: "If something, that people would have loved to keep, is taken away from them, then it is quite understandable that they might be sulking. It could be helpful if you let them know that you understand it is not so much fun for them now and that, nevertheless, things need to be done differently. At the systemic level, it could well be that a part – A in this case – is reacting to

---

not being acknowledged for what it has contributed. Especially when every mention of the previous manager is negative. When both the previous manager and the loose way of working can be recognised for what they contributed, it might be possible for the department to follow the new rules. By the way, do you have any idea what the value of the loose behaviour was to the system? To what did it contribute?"

After a short pause the director said that it is a department where people were very willing to respond to urgent customers issues and that this was something badly needed because of the nature of the company's customers at that time.

"If, systemically, nothing is drawing attention anymore, then the system can go forward, unfettered, into the future and do what needs to be done. If it seems unable to do so, then there might still be something else that needs attention. Probably, the people of the department know more than we think."

Temporary place

A common task for a manager is directing people. He needs to find a good match between what the organisation needs, what an employee can offer and what he thinks is needed. Many issues that end up with consultants, trainers and coaches are about this fine-tuning. As a result, the consultant can easily come to the edge – or fall into – the domain of the manager; you become a part of his system.

You need your own proper and clear place from where you can work in service of the whole. A place where you, without judgement, and multilaterally partial can be and act. Involved, but at a healthy distance. The best place for you to do this is a temporary place, outside the system.

From there you can respect and empower the system's own order. This demands that you always know and take your own modest and temporary place, from which you sense into the responsibilities that come with all the places in the organisation. How often do you find yourself being asked to do what the manager cannot or does not do? How easily can it happen that you weaken the manager by doing his job for him? What message does the team give when they warmly appreciate the external consultant who understands them so well and who facilitated the process so beautifully? That their manager does not understand and support them! And what is the consultant 'saying' when he accepts this appreciation? That he is, indeed, better than the manager!

Your job is to explore, in order to find out what weakens the system. As soon as you begin to clarify what could be the matter, with what the symptom might be related, or as soon as the necessary direction takes shape, it is time for you to withdraw. Helping systemically, is helping while passing by. You walk alongside for a very short while and then let go, trusting the system to continue under its own power. How difficult it is to take this unpretentious place. How many consultants, trainers, coaches and interim managers are secretly looking for applause in recognition of their expert input? And how is it, instead, to explore within yourself what it actually is that inclines you towards taking the place of one who knows better.

Being seduced

You have been asked to support a team and the employees tell you, confidentially, what they think of their manager.

Before you know it, you have become their counsellor and are no longer multilaterally partial: you look at the manager through the eyes of the team members. How on earth can you now help everyone involved to build a bridge together? On top of this, it is very likely that you weaken the team members by listening to them individually - collecting information with which you cannot do anything useful. You make yourself into the older and stronger 'brother' whom they hope will fix their problems for them. How would it be to say: "You may only tell me that which I am allowed to bring into the open with the whole team, including the manager, present. All the rest creates a barrier between you and me, and gives me a place in the team that is inappropriate and too important."

Restrained action

If, as an external adviser, you do what needs to be done by others within the system, by actively stepping in and intervening, you obscure symptoms. By doing so, it is no longer possible to see from where the symptoms originate or what they serve. Before you know it, the system becomes dependent on you, or other outsiders, and you prevent self-regulation from doing its work. Your contribution should be one of restraint: not so much to enter into someone else's system, but just to facilitate the other person, as if he were an outsider himself. Helping him to look at his own system and the place he takes within it; from a distance and without judgement. In this way, patterns can become clear and the organisation has the opportunity to learn to look differently at phenomena.

This restraint comes from realising that your biggest contribution is that you, looking from a distance, are able to see patterns. That, through your involvement, you can explain what happens within you, what you become aware of when making contact with the organisation. For a little while you walk along with people in the organisation, letting them feel your confidence that everyone will take his appropriate place and responsibility. If they don't do so, then this is only another symptom to be explored in the same open way and without any judgement. If this comes outside of your assignment, then you don't do it. Sometimes things need to get worse before they get better (a Chinese saying). Sometimes it is unavoidable that the system will react vigorously, in terms of the symptoms it manifests, before members of the system will listen to what it has to tell them. The consultant who does not want to help is the best help a system can get.

Help!

Usually, before you are called in to help, much has already happened in the organisation. They have established the problem, discussed it, often at great length and tried to solve it. Actually, you are lucky if you are asked to go in and have a look at what is really going on there. It is much more complicated if you are told: "This is the problem. This is, more or less, what we think you need to do ...? and roughly three weeks should be enough." *This actually happened, and the consul-*

SIEBKE KAAT AND ANTON DE KROON

*tant's answer was: "*Thank you for asking me in and for placing your trust in me. I think I understand the assignment. My line of approach is: how can all of you profit from what I am going to do? Can we dis-cuss that?" *This gave rise to a debate about how restrained interven-tion by the consultant would allow the system to regain its strength. The result was that the head of the department properly took his position, supported by three one-hour sessions with the consultant. The head found he could do the job himself. Not in three weeks perhaps and not according the predetermined plan, but from the strength of his own po-sition. And he gained the respect of his department.*

Later on, the consultant caught himself feeling rather too self-satisfied. How skilled he was to transform an everyday question into a systemic approach! What would they have done without his expertise? He re-alised that by thinking like this he put himself above the system. He was, once again, confronted by how difficult it is to stay only in your own place.

Systemic derailing

It is not always easy to stay on the systemic track, to always look and react from this open, unbiased attitude. You'll know, for certain, that you've left this attitude, when you start hurrying, getting excited, thinking you know the solution or judging people or situations. Or when you begin respond-ing to incidents or symptoms, without paying attention to the bigger pic-ture to which they point. If you feel yourself wanting to solve things, you surely are no longer working systemically. The more you feel like you are the expert concerning the content, or you judge yourself to be better than the people concerned, the more difficult it becomes, if not impossible, to intervene systemically. And if this should happen to you, would you be able to ask yourself, without judgement: *"What am I being loyal to when I act this way?"* Are you loyal to your professional training? Are you loyal to your place as the helper in your family system? Looking at yourself with-out judgement opens up the possibility to look at others in the same way.

4.4 Applied knowledge

- Where to start?
- Acknowledging the origin
- With an eye for the history
- Belonging and no-longer belonging
- Everyone in his own place in the order
- Group dynamics or system dynamics?

In chapter three we elaborated on the five fundamental systemic needs that need to be fulfilled in order to allow an organisation to function fully.

When asked to help (a part of) an organisation, your interest should include how well these needs are being met. Could the development of problems or symptoms be related to one or more of them? In this part, we tackle the question of how you can apply your knowledge of organisational systems in your everyday work.

Where to start?

There you are, sitting with the client, with all this systemic knowledge in your head. So many questions to ask, so many elements to explore and so much entering your awareness that it can make you dizzy. However, there seems to be an order, amongst the fundamental needs, that can guide you in exploring an organisational question.

When it is clear where the organisation, or that part of the organisation upon which you are focussing, comes from – its origin and history – and everything in there is being seen and acknowledged, this constitutes the foundation for the now. This is the reason why we begin by investigating that foundation.

The next step. Is it clear who and what belong at this moment, what connects them to each other and to the raison d'être of the organisation? Clarity about where you belong, when based on facts, creates safety and relaxation; then you do not need frantically to try to belong somewhere. 'Belonging', apparently, is a strong fundamental need that gives force and power to systems and their parts. So …? what are the subsystems and how are they embedded in the bigger whole?

Once the subsystems are clearly understood – for example departments or customers – and also their reasons to exist, then the moment is right to bring clarity to the order between all the parts. Each one taking his rightful place in the whole gives strength and energy, both to the whole and the parts. When the parts constantly do not want to restore the right balance between themselves, this is, most of the time, a symptom. Usually, it is a signal that one or more of the fundamental needs is not being met, or not yet met, or no longer met.

When particular changes or events are covered up – denial of 'history' – this immediately has an effect on belonging. It is difficult to connect to the now when the connection with the origin and the past (of the function, the department, the organisation) is weakening. Adopted children experience a similar problem when they are not allowed or able to acknowledge their origin. It is the same with mergers, when the names and logos of the constituent companies have to disappear and to be forgotten as soon as possible.

The past provides the foundation on which the now is resting. This can and must be seen.

When it is unclear where a person belongs, it shows itself at the ordering level. It is a well-known tension for workers team leaders or supervisors; they do not fully belong to their colleagues, but also not to the management. Often they fight for a clear place in the order, with a corresponding salary scale and function title. Because the belonging and, as a result of that, the place in the order, is so vague, things like the kind of company car, wages and privileges become increasingly important; all of them belong in the domain of the balance between taking and giving.

Unclear order produces behaviour that is, in effect, asking for the necessary clarity regarding the order. This seriously disturbs the balance between the people affected by the unclear order.

It seems as if a shortage in the field of one of the fundamental needs will, in the end, always have repercussions on the balance of taking and giving. But it is not there, in that balance, that the healing of the system will take place. This is the reason why, first of all, what needs to be explored is what happened to the other fundamental needs: where does the disturbance of the balance originate?

Guts and courage are needed to not follow the definition of the problem that is presented to you.

What could be helpful here is to see that, if the problem was that clear, the solution would have been found by now and they would not have needed you. Apparently, it isn't that easy. So your added value is, mainly, that you look further and differently.

You deliver your contribution in direct contact with representatives of the organisation. They are the ones who have to draw conclusions and take action. Make the process into a common exploratory expedition where you look together at the direction the compass is showing. Once that has become clear, the consultant departs, leaving, with the client, the compass and the direction it indicates.

To summarise: the order of exploration is a process of first zooming out and then zooming in. When the reason for coming into being, the origin and the history are seen and acknowledged, when it is clear who and what belongs and what each contributes to the whole, when the order amongst the parts is clear, it goes without saying that you will see the right balance between the parts of taking and giving. And, when all this is in place and still there are disruptions in the balance of taking and giving, then, usually, they are easily solved by the system members themselves, as the problems are not at the systemic level.

To illustrate, here follows a systemic exploration of some organisational questions related to the five fundamental needs.

Acknowledging the origin

Why don't we get on anymore?

A training bureau asked for help. The connection between the partners, who are also the founders, existed and did not exist at the same time. They had already tried all kinds of approaches, but it looked like the energy did not want to flow when they were gathered together. They

---

all experienced the tendency to cancel or cut their meetings short. They had already tried variations in procedures, times, places, chairmanship and frequency of their meetings; all to no avail.

They were asking for help; something had to change! Meanwhile the partners had reached the point where it would be a relief if the external consultant told them that it was no longer possible for them to meet in a pleasant and inspirational way.

The consultant, in search of something bigger, chose not to dig more deeply into their meetings. He made no judgements (they already had enough of their own).

He started by asking how they had come into being, what connected them at that time, why they had wanted to start this business together, what were their wishes, their ideals.

During this conversation the blinkers fell from their eyes. In the beginning, an especially important shared value was to be independent of each other (particularly financially); to be free to work in your own way, to develop yourself your way. How loyal they were, to these values, by allowing flow into their meetings only when they were focussed on a new assignment, but not when they discussed regular, operational affairs. They were quite surprised, too, that their original point of departure continued to be guiding them. And, in fact, as soon as they looked at it that way, they were able to let go of their judgements about it. They decided to limit the operational meetings to a minimum, keep them as short as possible and to let spontaneously-organised meetings occur, where a client's question would be the motive for coming together and inspiring each other as professionals. Acknowledging what is, without judgement, and revisiting their origins put the keys back in the hands of this team.

With an eye for the history

The takeover

A director complained about what he called the endless grumbling in his company: "It must stop; I'm fed up with it. It creates coldness and distance towards me. I've dismissed two people, but that hasn't helped."

The consultant saw the director's emotions. He looked injured, his good intentions misunderstood. An inner question arose: Who else feels injured? Misunderstood?

The consultant asked about the coming-into-being of the firm and what happened after that. The director: "We, a much larger German firm, took over a Dutch software company. The Dutch didn't like that. It became worse when the founder of our business was jailed? for fraud. As the director of both the German and the Dutch companies I told the Dutch employees: You should be pleased that you have been taken over; within a couple of years you would not have existed any longer." *And he explained to them that he had put a clear distance between himself and the founder.*

The consultant responded: "Apparently the Dutch firm was an attractive candidate for a takeover, for whatever reason. This fact seems to have been forgotten during all the ensuing hassle.

If the employees had not made the Dutch firm into what it was, 'Germany' would never have considered starting the takeover process. I can imagine that they feel aggrieved and might behave like obstinate children. Perhaps you can bring peace and quiet back by giving them the appreciation they deserve. It would be true, literally, if you said: 'If you had not existed, we could not have taken you over. Thank you for what you did.'"

With regard to the founder, the consultant said: "It looks like he has been erased from the history of the company. If that is the only thing the company does with him, it is denying that it has him to thank for its existence. As a founder he deserves a place, as a fraudster he has no place. This distinction matters."

SIEBKE KAAT AND ANTON DE KROON

Two months later:

In the office of the German director are three pictures of remarkable moments in the history of the Dutch company. Recovered from storage, sitting on a side table, is the original logo of the Dutch company, side by side with that of the new German company.

Belonging and no-longer belonging

The founder's place

The founder/owner has sold her company. She will receive a share of the profits for a specified number of years, but there is no longer a place for her. The new owner's question is: "How should I deal with the founder? She is inclined to drop in here; she is still in contact with some of the employees and, of course, they chat with her about the company. I don't feel free to do my work here. The employees feel uncomfortable when following my direction, because it is not the founder's direction. To put it briefly: how can I break free from the founder and guide the business in a new direction, without a huge conflict with the founder or some of the staff?"

The consultant: "The movement of your hands speaks volumes; you make gestures of brushing away. It looks as if you would rather throw her out. If I am right, she is, in some way, still inside the company." *It looks like the founder (and the company) live half in the new situation and half in the old. Very likely there was a farewell, but has the founder got a (permanent) founder's place? She inextricably belongs to the company, no longer as the owner but forever as the founder. Has there been an event or ceremony that gave her a place to say that she now belongs to the firm only as the founder; no longer as the boss? How would it be to thank her:* "Without you, this business would not have existed!" *And then to say to her:* "Let me take it forward my way, please, from the foundations you have laid. And, from a distance, look kindly at me, even when I do it differently ...".

Relief was immediately visible in the new owner. He no longer needed to brusquely eject the founder or forbid his employees to stay in touch with her. He could give her a clear place in this system, the place connected with its origin and history. Immediately he had ideas for how the company could honour this lady as its founder and builder. Perhaps a portrait on the wall, with her vision about the profession? Clearly, that would strengthen and inspire the business.

Everyone in his own place in the order

The place that gradually disappeared

A director asked for help from a consultant because intimidating behaviour was reported in his division. During their conversation, it became clear that employees had approached the director personally with a complaint about their team leaders.

The consultant: "What does that tell you? By coming directly to you they bypassed their own team leader, as well as the manager of the team leaders. What is happening here with the ordering?" *Searching for the reason for this behaviour the consultant and the director look back together. Not at individuals, but at facts: what has happened with the structure, with functions?*

They see that all the team leaders have worked in this division for a very long time. They are all very competent. Through looking back it also becomes clear that they have been fulfilling the team leader function for many years. Maybe that is what irritates the director most; it is exactly from these people that he expects a good example. But ... the function of team leader is going to be phased out. Everyone has known this for at least a year. When team leaders leave, they are not replaced. However, the team members are supposed, still, to do this work. They contribute to assessment interviews, chair discussions about work progress and make the schedules. They are in charge of daily operations.

The consultant: "Where do these people belong?" *The director:* "They don't belong to the management or to the group ..." "What will happen when the function disappears?" *The director:* "Then they will be just ordinary team members." "Is it realistic to suppose that both the members and the team leader might behave as if, all of sudden, they are equals? How can they erase their history, where one used to have a say in the salary of the other?" *The director is lost in thought.*

Let's return to what caused this conversation. The intimidating behaviour consisted of all manner of curt remarks and orders from the team leaders, that make it obvious to everyone that they are the ones in charge and they pull the strings. All of a sudden the director sees the connection. This is their way of making it very clear that their place, in between managers and employees, can not evaporate just like that. The consultant: "Apparently we have victims here, asking for attention."

Then they examine how the director can acknowledge what the team leaders have contributed during so many years and draw a line under their behaviour. Next they discuss the tricky issue of where labour law and the systemic view seem to be at odds with each other: is there still, somewhere in the system, an appropriate place for the team leaders?

Group dynamics or system dynamics?

Where group dynamics is a matter of constantly drawing attention, it often is, in reality, a matter of system dynamics.

Group dynamics are the combined actions of different people that usually have the wish or need to cooperate. Sometimes, friction between team members can negatively impact the team. Then interventions, at the level of group dynamics, are appropriate. These might take the form of expressing expectations, cleaning up old wounds, clarifying jobs and responsibilities, knowing each other's weak points and what makes individuals tick. When this approach does not lead to the desired outcome, it is quite likely that it is not at all about the group; it is about system dynamics.

System dynamics manifest in the behaviour of people. That is why, at first sight, it might look like something is wrong with a certain individual: "*He is the one to blame,*" or with a combination of individuals: "*They just don't get on."* But often people show something that is not theirs, but belongs to the system. They are only messengers, giving the signal that something within the system is asking for attention. An example: for a number of years there has been a lot of fuss about the vagueness of the role of the manager.

Now you are the new manager and you had expected to run into some problems in the beginning. In this case, however, it is neither your fault nor the fault of a previous manager. The reason is the place the managerial position has in the whole. As long as nothing changes there, every new manager appointed to this position will struggle.

If people do not invest in each other any more, or invest in a wrong or unpleasant way, the balance of taking and giving is disturbed. Often the primary tendency is to interpret it as being personal. When normal interventions by a manager prove insufficient, first of all we should look at whether the system is 'in order'. A powerful and vital system has a huge capability to regulate and restore itself. Asking for a group-dynamics intervention should immediately ring an alarm bell: what is stopping the system from self regulating? What prevents the manager from organising his team's group process in a healthy way?

4.5 Course of action

- Zooming out
- Focussed on functions and places
- Facts: the healing force of reality
- Awareness as an extra source

From your systemic attitude, holding your knowledge about the five fundamental systemic needs in your mind, you set to work. Here we describe typical working procedures that are characteristic of the systemic approach to issues in organisations.

Zooming out

The systemic consultant has traded in his microscope and magnifying glass for a camera with a fish-eye lens. Working systemically demands zooming out. Issues tend to be in the here and now, but your attention embraces the past as well. The issue is with a part? You pay attention to the whole.

Google Earth

Just like with Google Earth, the more you zoom out, the more you see the bigger picture. When using this programme to look at The Hague, you can choose to see the beach and the sea or not to see them. And that makes a difference in understanding how traffic will flow in that area.

You start by looking backward from now to what was earlier and from the part to the bigger whole. In both cases you are zooming out. By doing so you invite the manager to look in the same way, guided by the kind of questions with which you might now feel familiar. Do you recognise patterns from the past or patterns occurring at other places in the organisation?

Do the members of the team have their own, correct place? Do they know what their right to exist is? Did that change over time? In this gradual way you might arrive at the place where the system has put a red flag. This type of exploration immediately puts the tools in the hands of those responsible for reinforcing the system. Most managers are excellent at clarifying places and positions without any help, are very able to acknowledge what has happened and to relate the actual reason for existence with the original reason for coming into being.

Zooming out

The subject of the introductory meeting, with the director and the departmental manager, is about organising a day to encourage collaboration in the department. There, people are working too individually

---

and cooperating too little: the department has sixteen people fulfilling twelve functions.

The consultant, triggered by the difference between the numbers of people and functions, does not dive into the detail of their (un)cooperation, but asks the head of department: "What binds them together?" *To the consultant, it appears to be more their personal enthusiasm than the content of their work.*

The consultant, curious about possible patterns, enlarges the theme by asking the director: "What you see happening in this department, do you see something similar in other departments of which you are the director?" *But that is not the case.*

Casually, the director comments that she has known most of the people for quite a long time, but she's only been their boss for a couple of years. The consultant: "Where did they belong before this change; what was their place?" *Over a period of eight years, the department had been located in five different places. Each change of location was accompanied by a change of manager too.*

Aware that he is breathing quite high in his chest, as if a balloon is trying to lift him off his seat, the consultant says what suddenly occurred him: "For quite some time, the department has not had a stable place; as if it is floating around. Given that the functions fulfilled by the department are pretty diverse, where does the department actually belong? And if you work there, where is your home place?"

The consultant asks the director: "Are you happy with this department, with what it does and has to offer? Does it really belong to your domain, your area of accountability? If so, then you are the one who can give the department its place.

If not, then do your best to find a proper place for the department, or close it down!" *It was interesting to see how intently the manager was staring at the director, who said:* "I am sorry; I don't know what to do with this department. For the time being, it is as it is."

The consultant noticed the manager heave a sigh of relief the moment the director clearly took her place. By chance, she had created the clarity of the unclear.

The consultant, to the director: "What do you think? I suggest the head of department organises a session with his team around this theme: what is my history in this organisation and this department and what is my place here?" *– rather than focussing on getting them to cooperate more. The manager immediately agrees; the director also thinks it is a good idea. The consultant helps with preparing the session.*

Focussed on functions and places

In systemic consulting you focus on places and functions, not on the people who, 'accidentally', occupy those places at that moment.

Systemically, the person is not important; what matters is the place (that is given to someone) and what this place contributes to the whole. Next, you look at the connections and patterns between those places and the functions. For example between the various departments and between the organisation and its environment: its customers, financers, clients, suppliers and so on. You also look at the factual history of the functions, the departments and the organisation as a whole. You do not focus on feelings, or on the people who, by chance, are now in these places. This is an important difference between working systemically and working according to the principles of group dynamics.

The person is talking; it is the place that speaks

Often it is more important from which place you speak, than the words you say. When somebody says things that do not fit with his place, we tend to shrug our shoulders or we smile, thinking: "Who do you think you are to say that? You're too big for your boots." *For example, the child telling his parents that it is their bedtime; or the office-cleaner airing her opinion that the computers should be replaced.*

Only what is said from the right chair, which means from the right place, counts. Even if, in relation to the content, it is not a strong statement. When a prime minister decides that two ministries have to merge, then it will happen because he spoke from the appropriate chair. Usually it is not because of a natural and unavoidable consolidation.

As a systemic consultant you prefer to speak in terms of functions: the director, the research department, the head of the department, consumer group A and so on. You consciously avoid using people's names, in order to stay out of the personal field. This approach makes patterns more visible.

Them and us

Let's look at a general/technical support services function in a big company. It consisted of two departments, each with its own manager. One department operated at the central level, negotiating contracts with suppliers (security, catering, office furniture, plants, coffee machines and so on). The other fine-tuned supply and demand at a local level. For as long as anyone could remember both departments couldn't get on with each other. What was quite extraordinary – according to the preliminary talk with both managers – was that they all clicked with each other at a personal level. People knew how to find each other and could work things out together. But as soon it became a more formal procedure, a lot of relationship investment needed to be made in order to avoid trouble. This was a clear indication to leave the personal level immediately. Both managers, together with the consultant, described the history of their departments. This made it clear that the local team came into being earlier than the central one. Fact by fact the pattern appeared of energy and focus going increasingly to the central team. From this perception it wasn't odd that the 'local' team had to resist anything to do with 'central', because the order was being changed so stealthily.

It was decided to have a meeting with both teams. It was such a relief to the members that it was not to be about their personal relationships! To begin, both teams put into words the reason for the existence of the general and technical support services – as a whole. Subsequently, both teams were invited to formulate what was their own unique contribution and to draw, or otherwise bring into the picture, how they related to the other team and to the managers of their joint services.

This brought clarity and gave strength; all of them now knew, once again, the purpose of the services and also realised what were the unique contributions of their own team and the other team.

SIEBKE KAAT AND ANTON DE KROON

The order, too, became clear; it became evident that the place of the central team was, in no way, above the local team. It was more that the local team were able to point out to the 'central' team where collective and central frameworks and contracts would be of value and where they would not. This was a good basis to continue together.

Facts: the healing force of reality

> **"** *The truth is that which simplifies the world and not that which creates chaos.* **"**
>
> *Antoine de Saint-Exupéry*

Systemic consulting means being focussed on facts. By leaving opinions and feelings as they are, and exposing yourself only to the facts, patterns can become clear. Facts take away the emotional charge and create ease. Imagine a department with a turbulent past and too many loose ends. Like a smouldering fire, the old wounds flare up again and again. Proposing to look at it, is often greeted with the immediate reaction: *"We have done that so often; we just want it to stop; we don't want to go back over it again. The last time we did, so many of us were made out to be black sheep. Relationships were damaged even more. Wasn't that enough!"*

Apparently, it is common practice to look back, in the here and now, while living through the 'old' emotions and judgements. All that past frustration keeps everybody imprisoned, in a time and in events that are long gone. The past, however, cannot be repaired. Never. So the energy should not go there. The past can only be recognised and looked in the eyes. That is enough. Look at the facts and see that they caused real trouble for many people. Who, what and how is not important. For example, at times there was no manager, therefore people took that role, when it was neither their place nor responsibility and, therefore, they got things wrong. That is what the history is. And, systemically, it is not of any interest which person ended up in which role. Acknowledging that bigger forces were at work, with everybody being a 'plaything' of these forces, with very little influence, has a de-blaming effect. This is the way to recognise that it was difficult for everyone. It brings spaciousness and peace.

When the reality is too painful to see

After reorganising the local government authorities, the mayor said to the consultant: "He was superfluous; but we needed to find something for him. So we made him Senior General Policy Adviser. His reports are really quite good. But nobody reads them and nobody listens to him."

The consultant: "Yes that is what happens when a place is created just to get rid of a problem. It seems that the function was created without the new local authority needing it."

The mayor: "But we couldn't fire him; a man with so many good qualities."

The consultant: "What you did is worse than firing him. If there is no place for him, there is no place. That is the fact. And then you need to arrange an appropriate farewell. That would be better for the organisation and better for him."

Non-systemic interventions would become embroiled in the person and his qualities as an adviser and, before you knew it, he would have been sent on a report-writing course. Or they jump into group dynamics: *"Why doesn't the head of Department B read your reports? Maybe the two of you need to sit together and discuss how it works between you both and how you can make better use of each other."* Intervening systemically supposes that obvious, more-common interventions have already been made – adjusting when someone doesn't function well, or clarifying expectations and tasks – or have proved irrelevant. And then it is unnecessary to focus there. Intervening systemically asks you to 'unlearn' the approach of exploring individual feelings and to learn to ask for facts related to origin, history, belonging and order.

Awareness as an extra source

> **"** *It is only with the heart that one can see rightly;*
> *what is essential is invisible to the eye.* **"**
>
> *Antoine de Saint-Exupéry*

Systemic consulting requires being very conscious of your own perceptions. What is happening to me as I come into contact with this system, this building and these people?

In order to be of service to an organisation you adopt a completely open, unbiased attitude. It is not you entering the organisation, but the organisation entering you. What then happens to you? What, within yourself, enters your awareness?

Entering

A big, new building. High halls, large spaces. It houses many training institutes and colleges. Many different colours, forms and materials. It feels like a marketplace: a place to meander through, but also somehow lost. I feel insignificant. How do I find my way? I can't help feeling insecure. If I were to sit here all day, would someone come, in the evening, and tell me: "We are closing now"?

All, really all, the doors have strong closers. I have to push hard to open a door. It closes itself immediately behind me. I notice, with a sigh of relief, that it does not slam. Nowhere can I see an open door. Do they want to keep me out of here? Or do they want to offer me security and privacy?

Am I somebody or nobody here? I feel myself becoming insecure when this question arises in me. I decide to be somebody, which makes me walk briskly. This causes me to feel better than my surroundings. Mmm, that was not my intention either ...

Will any of this be recognisable in the issue they are about to discuss with me?

What happens to me here?

A hall, 30 × 15 metres, one corner filled with coloured chairs. This was the place the client chose for getting acquainted. Five storeys of open space.

What is happening to the consultant? He's feeling uneasy. How can he find his place in this room? Does this theme, of place and room, maybe play on other fronts too? So much air … is something needing air in this organisation? When you are using this space everybody can see you. Is something waiting for attention? Is the openness here too big for something to dare to come forward? Must everything here be seen? How can you find protection here?

During the meeting the consultant asked, among other things: "Is it easy or difficult to show yourself in this organisation? And is that appreciated or is it better to work silently?" *The client reacted with surprise:* "That is a good question, but what made you ask it? On the one hand we are a very transparent organisation with people from every walk of life. Everyone can see your rank and, consequently, your salary. That is how you can show yourself. But you better not stick your neck out."

4.6 Systemic exploring

- Symptoms: dire necessity
- Problems are solutions
- Looking beyond the symptoms
- A closer look at common symptoms

Any behaviour, any pattern that persistently stays, has meaning for the organisational system. If it didn't, it would have disappeared long ago, or an 'ordinary' intervention would have relieved it.

Sometimes, people want to get rid of such behaviour because it has a cost attached to it. But, before it can leave, its message must be understood. Just like your favourite teddy bear: you only can let it go after you have shown everyone how important it has been to you. Then you can leave it behind as a symbol of times gone by. But how do you search for the systemic roots of behaviour and patterns that, up till now, were only a burden?

Symptoms: dire necessity

We'll repeat it once more: a living system flourishes when in tune with the outside world and enjoying sufficient provision for its systemic needs of belonging (including origin and history), order and the balance of taking and giving. If this is not the case, then something – potentially danger-ous – happens to the survival mechanisms of the system. Self-regulation kicks-in with solutions that, on the one hand give an immediate answer to the current problem and, on the other hand are a cry for help – because 'something' is asking for attention. We experience this plea as a problem. But you also can look at it as the system helping: a solution born out of the need of a systemic principle that, in some way, has been neglected. The symptom is asking for attention for the neglected principle. The solution is hidden in the symptom. But how do we find it? From Matthias Varga von Kibéd comes the saying: *"Headache is not lack of aspirin."*

Problems are solutions

Searching for the function of unwanted behaviour in your organisation means searching for its source. Acknowledging that it exists for a good reason, generates the password to walk the right path. Just as in some countries you may use a motorway only when you have bought a permit for your windscreen.

Solving a problem is never a struggle against something. It is always being respectful to what is served by this particular human behaviour. By seeing and acknowledging the underlying cause, the behaviour itself no longer needs to be so strongly present. After all, for the system, it is only an indicator, no more. What is being experienced as a problem, turns out to be a systemic solution.

Those who carry the burden of the problem really need to take the time to explore what the signals might mean. It is stunning how quickly a few good systemic questions and remarks can lead you to the core of the issue.

Why the usual method fails

When people don't call each other to account, this can be a way to avoid saying something too harsh, that might permanently damage relationships, or cause some or all of the system to fall apart. Looked at this way, this symptom proves to be a good solution for an apparently unsafe situation. Also, and immediately, it provides tools to explore its cause. Did, for example, arguments arise through calling colleagues to account? Have people been damaged, relationships broken? Did the team fall apart? These phenomena could well be the system protecting itself against the next separation. Another question that pops up is whether the leader of the team is taking his place as the guardian of the whole. When he does not, there is no safety net. Then it is quite understandable that people don't take the risk of starting arguments that might end up with them being excluded. Not withstanding the fact that there is a problem in the order, and that the past still asks for attention, the symptom of not calling each other to account is also a solution. It ensures that the team remains a team. Providing training in 'How to call each other to account' would not deliver a solution, because the core of the problem cannot not be solved by the application of skills or techniques.

Looking beyond the symptoms

Many problems are phrased in terms of a disturbed balance in taking and giving:

- People do not invest anymore: cutting corners; nine-to-five mentality; not taking responsibility; excluding; silo mentality; everyone for himself and so on.

- People give too much: they burn out; feel overworked; take on tasks that don't belong to their function and so on.

- People take too much: sick leave; fraud; theft; falsifying expenses; taking extended breaks and so on.

- People 'give' in negative ways: gossip; harassment; criticism; aggression; saying yes and doing no and so on.

Before you know it, you have entered, deeply, into individuals' issues and what moves them to do what they do. As we stated earlier, unfulfilled fundamental needs always manifest in a disturbed balance.

This is exactly the reason that a systemic exploration of symptoms does not attempt to get to the bottom of the disturbed balance between individuals or departments, but focuses on origin, history, belonging and order.

So ... a first question could be:

- When did it start and what happened at that time?

Subsequent discussion explores how the symptom is related to the organisation:

- Does the symptom exclusively manifest in this part, or can you see it in more parts of the organisation?

- Did something similar happen before?

- What benefit does the symptom bring; what is its value, its function?

- What would be missed if this problem, this symptom, no longer existed? Who would pay a price?

- Which functions or groups carry the burden now? Who benefits?

When regular interventions haven't worked, it often happens that just exploring the systemic needs rings a bell with the client. A meaningful silence occurs, or people start telling relevant stories. In this way, a persistent symptom can finally show what stands in the way of turning people's goodwill and personal commitment into success.

A closer look at symptoms

Here follow some very common symptoms, accompanied by useful systemic questions that help identify some solution directions. There are far more of these questions and remarks than we will mention here. We just want to show some possible directions; ways in which you might want to think.

The questions invite you to look for patterns; without judgement. They explore the value or the function of those patterns, now or in the past. These are questions that lead to zooming out and, by doing that, to a different view of things.

Silo culture

A big company; branch offices all over the country. In addition to the local and regional branches there are many different units, department and projects: production, technical, customer relationship, international business, maintenance and so on. Some parts suffer from what is often called a silo culture. Other parts actively maintain their silo status and see more profit than loss in doing so.

- When did the silos emerge? What happened at that time?
- Are the silos isolated or do groups of silos exist?
- Were there connections between (all/some of) the silos in the past?
- What would be completely lost if the silos were to become one big whole?
- Is there a whole? Do connections with the whole exist?
- What connections are desirable? Under what conditions could they come into being?

Shirking one's responsibilities

It's the day before Christmas and, in a nursing home, while vacuuming, one of the staff knocks over a resident's television. The TV is ruined; these things happen. Watching TV is the only activity this resident can do. There could hardly be a worse day for this to happen: where are they going to find a new television on Christmas Eve? The family members find a temporary solution, but they expect the nursing home to provide a new TV very quickly. That, however, seems unlikely: *"No, I am not in charge of that.*

You'll have to ask the team leader." "No, not me, it is the manager's respon-
sibility." "We'll have to wait and see how much the insurance will refund."
"We do not have a budget for this." "The bookkeeper is the right person to
decide, but he is on sick leave." Ignorance, indignation and disappoint-
ment are everywhere.

- What is the price of taking responsibility here?

- What is being served by saying: *"I am not in charge of this."*

- Residents enter the home because they are unable to live on their
  own anymore. The family cannot take care of them and hands the
  issue over to the home. Staff members can no longer make autono-
  mous decisions. What would happen if this repeating pattern was
  broken?

- What is the origin of this home. Nursing or being a 'home'?

- When the staff and family members are looking at each other, who
  is looking at the residents? What might be too painful to look at?

Staff turnover

It is a consultancy for international business contracts. In the Africa division they have to contend with the remarkably large turnover of younger
lawyers. The majority stay only a couple of years. Their company cars have
already been upgraded; flying business class is now standard. But these
improvements do not reduce the turnover. Exit interviews offer no insight
into why they leave so soon. Other divisions do not have this problem.

- What is the price of staying: for individuals; for the division?

- What is kept alive by the younger lawyers leaving?

- Who wanted to stay, but had to go?

- What was the reason for this Africa division coming into existence?

- What happened to the founder and to the first director of this division?

- Are there functions that do not have this problem?

- When did the phenomenon start and what happened to the following elements, around that time: functions, advice and contracts, the director, the consultancy itself, African countries, customers?

Us against them

It happens, quite often, that a workers union and a director stand against each other. The phenomenon of 'us against them' can frequently be seen in organisations with an office staff and a field organisation. Or between management and the shop floor. There is an atmosphere of blaming, being misunderstood. Time and again everyone can see how it 'really' is: the other party is against us, is not open enough, or is always interfering in things they don't know anything about and that are none of their business at all.

- What is the value of this divide?
- Would there still be 'us' without 'them'?
- Is each one of them connected to a different key value of the company?
- When not looking at each other, where do they look?
- To what do you become disloyal when no longer being 'against'? What would this cost?
- Did anyone ever try to build bridges? What has become of them?
- If the gap was bridged, who would react with joy? Who would find it unbearable and immediately try to re-establish it?

On the way to a burn out

It is not normal: everybody is working too much, too hard and, already, for such a long time. There are 'good' reasons: deadlines to be met, an important customer threatening to leave, the vacancy for which no good candidate can be found and so on.

- Are there places without burned-out people?
- Whose place is weakened by others doing too much?

- What status has a burn out? What do you gain by having no boundaries?
- If the impossible is being asked, who is asking it?
- What do you gain by doing an impossible job?
- How do groups of customers perceive this organisation? As an organisation delivering what they promise, or an organisation that is doing its best and must not be criticised?
- What is the price for the organisation or department that does set boundaries, where people are accountable, meet their commitments, create realistic goals?

It just won't work

It looks so beautiful, the new product. It has been thought through, has superb specifications, market research suggests there is a need for it and it is keenly priced. It was launched with a well-proven, successful campaign, but nobody is buying it.

- For whom or what would it be a disgrace if the product was a success?
- If the founder was here, would he be happy with the new product?
- If the history could look at the new product, what might it tell us?
- Suppose the creators had forgotten to put 'something' in the product. What could that be?
- What could possibly be using this failure to ask for attention?
- Who or what would pay a price if the product became a success?

Harassment

It seemed to be such a nice, assertive and open group. Yet a survey shows a substantial number of the people experience intimidation, discrimination and harassment, by colleagues but also by team leaders. The management find it impossible to put a finger on the cause. When they fix it in one place it just pops up somewhere else, in slightly different clothes.

- Which order is exerting its influence here? Or, in other words, what wants to be acknowledged? Old/young, seniority, one function/ another function, social class, immigrant/native, craftsmanship, experience …?

- Among which functions/people/groups does it not exist?

- What would change, in the formal ways of belonging, if harassment stopped? What would change in the informal ways of belonging? What would be the price?

- What would it mean for the order if people stopped harassing others? What would be the price? Who would pay it?

- If crossing personal boundaries is the pattern, do you see it in other places in the organisation?

- What is this pattern's function for the organisation?

- What would happen if everybody limited himself to only his function and his tasks?

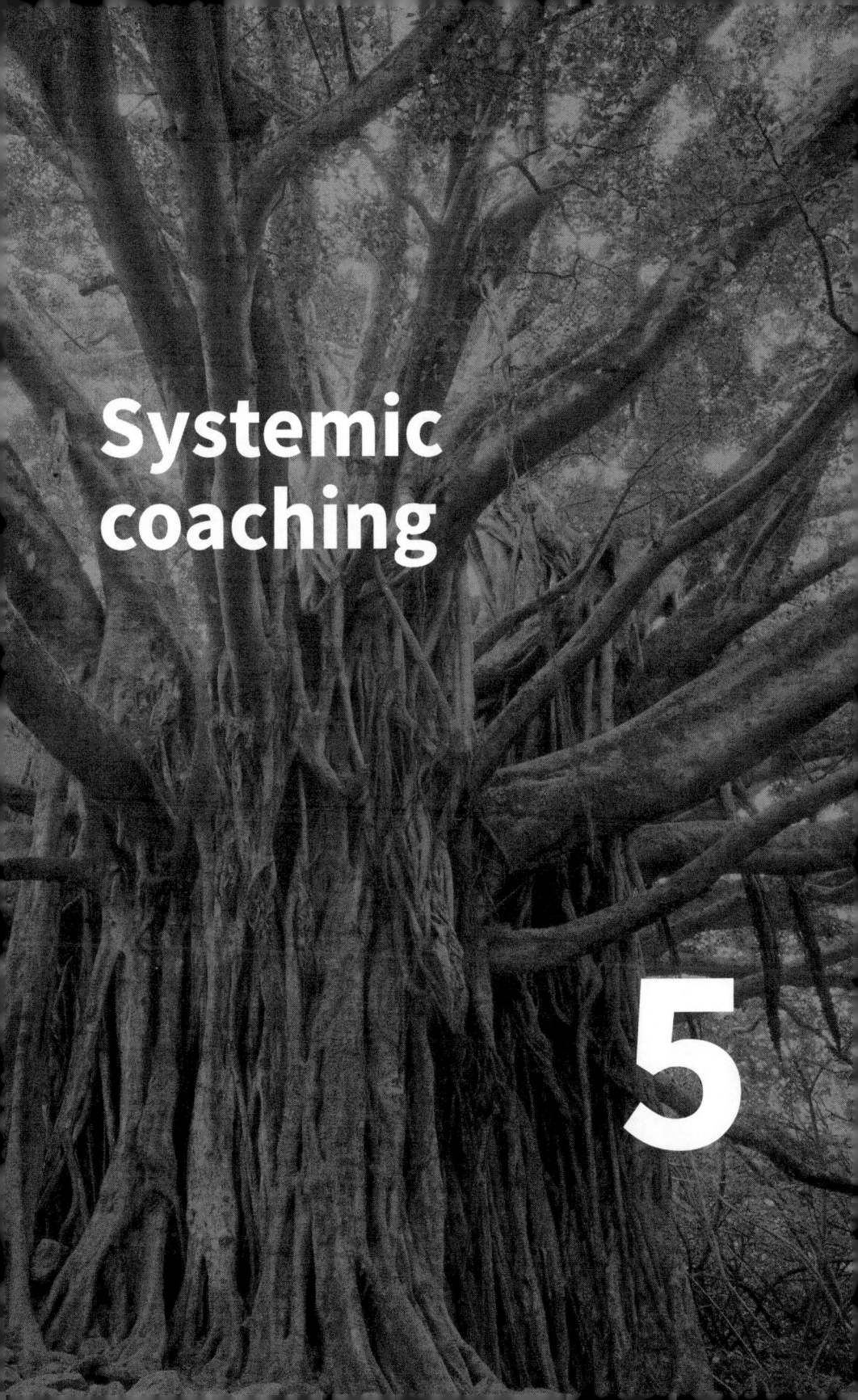

Systemic coaching

5

Introduction

- Characteristics of systemic coaching
- Contracting
- Finding the root of the problem

Common themes in coaching

- Repeating patterns
- Systems confusion
- There's something about this place ...
- Preservation and renewal
- Letting go by recognising

Questions to contemplate

- Questions about the coach
- Questions about the client

5.1 Introduction

This book is about organisations as living systems and, in particular, how an external consultant can contribute, in a systemic-phenomenological way, to what a system needs. We are making this short excursion, from the world of consulting to the world of coaching, because many consultants also coach individuals around work-related issues. So far, in this book, we have strived to elaborate on every aspect that a systemic consultant might encounter. However, we do not have that in mind for this chapter. It is merely an initial and global exploration of what turns coaching into systemic coaching.

Characteristics of systemic coaching

Systemic coaching has several characteristics:

- The systemic coach, just like the systemic consultant, uses his awareness as information. Completely open and without judgement, he exposes himself to what arises in him through his contact with the client and the bigger whole to which the client belongs.

- He always works from his systemic attitude, conscious of the fact that he contributes best by seeing everyone and everything in the context of the whole. He does not join in the client's judgements about colleagues, the management or the organisation. He does not want to solve anything. Together with his client he wants to look at what appears from the system, what happens to the client in that organisational system and what, potentially, the client could do to take his place in a better way. He resists the temptation to portray himself as the expert, the helper or the saviour of the client or the system as a whole.

- Always, he puts any question about an individual employee in the context of the whole of the system. It is for this whole that he works.

- With his systemic radar, he permanently scans all the parts and the system as a whole. He is on the alert for anything to do with the belonging or excluding of parts, the order, the place his client is taking (or has been given) and the history of that place.

- He is attentive to what is repeating itself, both in the person and work of the client, and in the organisation within and for which he is working.

- His efforts are aimed at enabling the client to discover the dynamics of which he is a part.

- He regards problems as symptoms that just want to show, systemically, where the shoe pinches. So the content of a client's story rarely contains the real issue: it is only the wrapping around the gift of a systemic phenomenon. The coach should regularly ask himself this question. For what is this problem a good solution?

Contracting

Systemic coaching is oriented at getting the client to look from a systemic perspective at his question, his place and his situation. By doing so, he might recognise his personal patterns in 'his' organisational systems. Or he might be able to see that some of his behaviour expresses his loyalty to someone or something from his family of origin. By looking without judgement, transcending patterns can become clear. Sometimes one session is enough, sometimes more are needed. But it is the client who decides this, not the coach. The coach's place is beside the client. He does not guide the client, he only facilitates a process in which the client can look at his situation in a different way and can then act differently. By deciding for himself, how often and with what frequency sessions will take place, the client takes the lead. The systemic coach lets go of that.

Finding the root of the problem

In systemic coaching the first question is, always, in which system will we find the root of the problem. Does what is being experienced as a problem relate more to the person or more to the organisation? Or is it, by chance, related to both systems?

When it appears to belong more to the person, systems confusion might be the issue: someone in the organisation is behaving as he used to behave at home, when he was younger. Irrespective of his work environment, he takes his place – in relation to his colleagues and management – in the same way he did in the past with his siblings and/or parents. Often, the client recognises the problems it causes and has experienced similar problems in previous work situations. Whenever someone else, temporarily or permanently, took his place, that newcomer did not experience these problems; predecessors did not encounter them either. These are signals that the issue originates more from the family context than the organisational.

An indication that the problem is likely to be more related to the organisation is when the client tells you that what is happening to him is really strange. He hardly knows or does not know it at all. Further inquiry can reveal that others, in similar places, run into similar issues. Then it is very likely that it belongs to the organisation. A different person, in the same place, would almost certainly experience the same problem.

And then of course there is the mix of both. The organisational and the personal; with their own typical patterns both, somehow, attract each other. The pattern of one fulfils a need of the other and vice versa.

You might ask yourself the question, to what extent is the choosing of a job, or the choosing of an employee, an act of free will? Sometimes it looks as if each is being pulled towards the other like magnets. Magnets that believe they are acting autonomously!

5.2 Common themes in coaching

People, knocking at a coach's door with work-related problems, usually express what bothers them in terms of a personal dilemma or issue. In the following part of this chapter we give ten examples of such issues and classify them within overarching systemic themes:

- Repeating patterns
  - I know how it should be done here!
  - I have been far too busy.
- Systems confusion
  - Here, I feel like a little girl.
- There's something about this place ...
  - I am not successful here.
  - I have to leave, again.
  - I am not seen.
- Preservation and renewal
  - They don't want me anymore.
- Letting go by recognising
  - I don't want this any longer.
  - I want to leave.
  - I don't like it anymore.

Now we'll share a few examples from our own coaching practices; here and there with a short theoretical comment.

Repeating patterns

Most of the time people are convinced that they behave according to the situation they are in. It is cold outside; therefore I put on a coat. When someone is wearing a coat almost every day, even in midsummer, then you might ask yourself whether this behaviour is really related to the situation, or if it is more an unconscious, compulsive repetition, irrespective of what the situation demands. This is what we call a repeating pattern.

A repeating pattern can manifest as a client being strongly inclined to leave, or not to take the place in the system that is there for him. This can show in various ways. For example, by taking a position on the sideline; leaving the organisation; taking the boss's place or – if he is the manager – taking a place among the employees. Often these are old mechanisms the client 'learned' in his family of origin. It is also possible that his behaviour repeats the behaviour of his predecessor – who occupied the same place. In both situations the behaviour stems from (unconscious) loyalty (see chapter three). Loyalty to a pattern from his family can ensure that, time and again, a client ends up in a similar, unwanted, situation – whatever his job or employer.

An inner attitude of I know better than my boss points to the pattern of parentification. Someone acting from this dynamic, this pattern, has, in his inner self, left his own place and taken a place above him. The concept of parentification comes from family system therapy and describes when a child takes the place of a parent. When coaching such a person, it is most helpful to let him retake his place and, from there, acknowledge the organisation's leaders in their places.

I know how it should be done here!

The manager explained that he did not feel understood by his director, although he frequently presented new ideas to him. Disdainfully, he added: "And he is one of those directors who insists that his door is always open."

SIEBKE KAAT AND ANTON DE KROON

The coach is apprehensive; immediately he doesn't want to accept or follow the manager's judgement. He registers, in himself, his reaction to the criticism of the director, his tendency also to judge ... if not the director, then the manager – one of those people who always know better. Additionally, he registers the manager's attitude: his chin pointing upward, one hand making a gesture of waving aside, his tone of voice. He comes across as arrogant. And the thought arises: does he want to be coached or does he want to take the director's place ...?

The coach registers all these things and simply lets them go. Realising that the theme of 'ordering' is coming up here, he asks the manager: "What do you think? Would it be good for the organisation if the two of you changed places?"

Well, to him, changing permanently seemed to be asking a bit too much. But for a period of time he would love to do it; to show how the job should be done.

The coach offers some systemic clarification: "That is not your place. As long as you don't recognise the director as your boss and don't want to see what you can contribute from your proper place, there will never be a place for you in this system."

The manager found that hard to swallow. Then he asked how he could do it differently.

The coach: "The answer is to do what is appropriate for your place, or to find a place where you can do what fits you. What fits the place you have now, is making it clear to the director that you respect his authority and decisions. If the director is interested, once in a while, you could go and see him and let him know, without any obligation on his part, how you see your business. And I mean this exactly as I say it: your business, not the business. This would make it possible for the director, perhaps, now and then, to ask for your opinion. Then, clearly, it is no longer about his position. What you could do, also, is find a place in another system. Or is it that you really like the place of the employee who knows better than his boss?"

I have been far too busy

The client had been far too busy. She took on responsibilities that were not hers, but she was so involved with the work and her clients that she didn't see any other way. She had already taken a course in time management and been coached to be more assertive and set her boundaries. But all of this had only short and temporary effects. She was tired, so tired.

The coach looked at her closely. Yes, indeed, she did look tired and, at the same time, it looked as if she did not want to let go of one single gram of her burden. It seemed more as if she was longing for a pat on the back. From whom might she want to receive it? From whom had she taken over the burden? Perhaps, much earlier in her life?

The coach tried to explore whether there was a pattern and said: "Carrying your own weight strengthens you; carrying someone else's weight wears you out!" *The client agreed with this and immediately said:* "Yes. But if nobody else takes responsibility, then I have to jump in. If I don't, then things will go wrong for our clients and they are so vulnerable already ...". *The coach, on the trail of the repeating pattern:* "Do you recognise, at some time in your youth, that you took on what belonged to someone else, because you were worried about what would go wrong if you didn't?" *The client fell silent. Clearly, she was going back in her life. She said, after a while:* "I had no option, my mother was too drunk to take care of my little sister."

Systems confusion

People – unconsciously – can be inclined to take the place, in their work system, that they took in their family-of-origin system. In certain situations they might behave as if they are in a their family-of-origin system. Here, as a coach, you need all your systemic antennae: does the client respond as if other people, or you, are a family member? What pattern of interaction, from the family system, is being repeated in the organisational system?

Here, I feel like a little girl

This woman notices, in some way or other, that she 'shrinks' when she is in contact with her manager.

She starts stuttering, feels like a small child – which she hates – all the more so as she does not experience herself this way when in contact with other professionals. During the coaching it became clear to her that it happened more often when in contact with women in senior positions, rather than men. The coach, also female, registered what was happening to her in her contact with the client. She felt inclined to protect the client, to help her. As if the client was inviting or evoking the mother role in her. The link she made to the mother-daughter relationship hit the client like a ton of bricks. She detected that, indeed, she became a dependent child in her contact with female managers and senior colleagues. Once she realised that this had everything to do with her relationship with her mother and nothing to do with her manager, she was able to see the manager as just the manager. The systems confusion was lifted ... but the relationship between her and her mother is a different story.

There's something about this place ...

Perhaps it has nothing to do with a repeating pattern or systems confusion, but still the client does not know why he is not successful in his place. A characteristic of behaviour that is more related to the place – and therefore to the system – than to the person, is that the client does not recognise it at all. Neither from other work places nor from his personal background. For you, as a systemic coach, this signal is confirmed by the fact that, to your surprise, this client, even though he has all the qualities, tasks and accountability that go with his place, doesn't perform well. Together, you start exploring what could be wrong with 'his' place. Here are three variations of there's something about this place.

It is not working out for me here

"It is impossible for me to be successful here. My usual qualities just don't seem to be enough. I feel so insignificant, while it is a solid and appropriate function. I can't put my finger on the problem. I have never experienced this kind of thing before."

Exploring the history of that place is revealing, especially since the client doesn't recognise it at all. It looks like the place is not available for him; systemically speaking, a predecessor is still keeping the place. Some-body who has physically left the place but to whom people are still, at heart, loyal. And perhaps the predecessor has not yet let go of the place himself. An acknowledgment farewell ritual, initiated by the client, could be helpful. "Thank you for occupying this place before me; could you please hand it over to me now?" *(Could be done with his actual colleagues present.)*

I have to leave, again

"I deliberately chose my function in this team, but somehow I feel in-clined to leave again; I can't settle here."

This sign is a good reason to check if something happened with the predecessors in this place. Who else left? Who must not or could not stay? Who left, suddenly, without recognition?

Together with his manager and colleagues, a client can look back at what happened to his predecessors in the role. What is it that seems to have turned this place into a systemically-burdened one? In such cases, something has been lost or has not been acknowledged. For example, tasks have been taken away from the function, a restructuring in the or-ganisation, the denial of someone's contribution in this place and so on. And here, too, acknowledgement of the past is the key to unlocking change.

I am not seen

"They permanently pass me by and 'forget' me. I keep explaining the responsibilities of my function, in which meetings I want to participate and what I need to be kept informed about, but it just doesn't seem to register with them. I don't understand it at all; people are very happy that I'm here and honestly try very hard not to forget me."

These are signals for the coach that the function appears to have no weight, as if it has no foundation, no right to exist, is not embedded in the system. Often you can see somebody still being successful in such a place, somehow. Perhaps by privately investing a great deal in personal relationships, and this, in some way, grants him his responsibilities, instead of the place doing this automatically. All supernumerary staff, people who have lost their places but still belong ("*You may stay, but no longer as a manager*") or people in fabricated roles, know the phenomenon of the (systemically) non-existent place. You (still) belong, but have no place. What is needed here? Find a proper place … or say goodbye. It might feel appropriate for you, as a coach, to give a rough sketch of the tension between the completely different world of systemic perception and behaviour and the one of labour laws, social controls and the like.

Preservation and renewal

Systems want everything and everyone that belongs, or belonged, to be acknowledged and receive and take a clear place. Systems, and the environment in which they function, change continuously: because parts change, because the outside world changes. Reciprocity, between the preservation of what is so familiar to the system and adaptation to new realities, reinforces the system. However it is not an easy process, to continuously find a new balance between the extremes of falling apart and rigidly sticking to the old.

They don't want me anymore

In a child therapy practice, the wish of one of the therapists, to follow a new path, was critically discussed. His choice was influenced by what one could call 'reaching the child via the parents'. This therapist became more and more interested in this approach, also for the practice, and it was a completely new way. To the other therapists it felt a bit strange, so they kept on questioning him about his basic assumptions, but no answer he gave was good enough. They had been busy with this issue for such a long time and the group grew increasingly irritated.

One Sunday afternoon the therapist was talking with a systemically-trained friend who said to him: "The others feel that you are being un-faithful to them. They so dearly want you to belong to them, the way you always used to." *This enabled the therapist to see the group's criticism differently.*

He was confronted with the question of whether he really wanted to face the fact that, for him, a time might come when he would say farewell to his colleagues. And he also imagined how it might look if a new form of therapy found a place in the current practice. Anyway, he now understood and appreciated the passion underneath their criticism of him. It was a cry for clarity about his connection; a question about whether he wanted to connect the new to what was already there.

Letting go by recognising

A coaching session often starts with the wish or urgent need for something to change. Perhaps something has to go. Someone wants to get rid of something and replace it with something new. For example, the pressure of work must disappear and relaxation should replace it.

The very best way to keep something is to passionately try to get rid of it. Acknowledging its value is the key to a change in attitude. What is acknowledged for its contribution, usually coexists well with the choice for something new.

I don't want this any longer

A social worker became desperate because he couldn't keep his clients out of his thoughts. He was always busy with them. He couldn't let them go. He had already tried a symbolic ritual: putting them in a garbage bag and placing it outside his front door. But to no avail.

The coach connected himself with the phenomenon of always being busy with clients and a question arose about another system: "Who might be proud of you, seeing you so engaged with your clients?"

After quite a while, the client speaks about his father, who impressed on him, during his childhood, that no job is ever finished; one can always do more.

The coach remarks: "All of a sudden, while you're telling me this, your face becomes more relaxed, very different from before. And I notice that I also get calmer."

The client: "Yes, my father is a very enthusiastic, involved person, although sometimes he can come across as a bit compulsive."

The coach: "And you? Do you recognise yourself there? Maybe the time has come to thank your father for what he taught you. Now, as an adult, you could start exploring new ways, without devaluing your father's message. It is good to show your involvement and your enthusiasm, but in your own way."

I want to leave

It was becoming more and more difficult at work. He didn't like it anymore; he'd felt this way for a long, long time. He said: "The job doesn't amount to anything. Colleagues? Well, no more than superficial contact. I prefer to avoid meetings. All in all, it gnaws away at my self-confidence. I don't want to be here anymore. But, somehow, I can't leave. Something holds me in its grip."

The coach noticed that his heart and awareness were leaning towards the place the other wanted to leave. Was it asking for attention?

The coach said: "It might sound odd, but I suggest you try loving the place you want to leave. What did it give you and could you be appreciative of that? What did you contribute in that role? In order that you might really leave that place, do you grant the organisation the right to all that you gave, whatever they might do with it? Can you take and leave everything exactly as it is; both the pleasant and the unpleasant things?"

While saying this the coach, all of a sudden and for the first time, saw a kind of shine come over the client's face.

He continued: "Now that you recognise what is happening, it could be that it's not just you who wants another place, it might also be that the place wants to let you go … because the exchange between the two of you has come to an end." *The client gave a deep sigh.*

I don't like it anymore.

The client doesn't feel at ease in the team; he continually clashes with the team leader. He feels connected with only three of his eight colleagues.

With the others he has nothing in common. Time and again he does his best to contribute and time and again he is unhappy with the response he gets. And now the annual team-building session is approaching. For years he helped to prepare it, feeling responsible for planning interesting, useful sessions. This time he is not involved in the preparations. He is at his wit's end. He has a bad feeling in his stomach about the day and fears it will be just a lot of hassle and difficulty. "Please, tell me what I should do."

The coach realises it has to do with 'place'. What is his place in the team? How can he take it? Then he falls into the trap of being the one who knows better by saying: "There are some colleagues with whom you feel at ease. Why don't you make sure you sit next to them?"

As always when you try to solve someone else's problem, your suggestions are swept aside. "No, that won't work because …"

I should have thought of that myself, the coach realises, noticing also that he has listened too much to the content of the story, instead of listening 'through' the content to the deeper-lying message.

The coach took his time, thought about how, on the day, all the team members would enter the room and choose a place to sit. Then this idea arose: "Imagine the day in your head. Make a picture of all of you, there together. Where are you sitting?"

Immediately the answer came: "I'm sitting at the edge, looking outward."

The coach: "What if you were to take that place completely, exactly as it is: at the edge, looking outward. As if that is the way you take part. As if that is your place, then and there. How would that be?"

A sigh escaped from the client and his face relaxed: "Sometimes it is so good to just admit how it is. It brings peace."

5.3 Questions to contemplate

The systemic coach has many questions. They keep running through his mind. He is barely interested in the answers. The questions are more like reminders of an open way of looking, of exploring possibilities. They are questions to muse, questions that need to simmer slowly. He asks them about himself and also about the client. Here are some examples.

Questions about the coach

- Am I equally able to find a place in my heart for the client and everybody around him?

- How do I make and keep the client responsible for his own learning? In order to achieve this, what do I need to let go of?

- What place do I love to take? What pattern might I easily repeat in my contact with the client? How is it, to be (just) really supportive instead of guiding? What do I gain when the client is grateful to me? What happens to the client when he attributes his development to me? How do I avoid becoming more important than the client's manager? How do I avoid becoming more important than the client himself, in his process of development? What can help me to avoid the pitfalls; what support do I need here?

Questions about the client

- What place does the client usually take in relation to the management, to colleagues, to customers? What happens to me when I'm in contact with this client? What might this tell me about what is going on in him? What pattern might repeat itself between the two of us?

- What is the origin of the behaviour the client doesn't want anymore? What benefit did this same behaviour give him earlier in his life? If his behaviour is an expression of loyalty, whom or what would, maybe unconsciously, feel happy about that?

- Does the client recognise what manifests here as an 'old' pattern of his/hers, from earlier situations, work or private?

- What happened to the place before the client took it?

- Is the issue with the client recognisable as a pattern of the organisation?

- For what is the problem actually a good solution?

- What might be lost if the problem no longer existed?

Contributing to healthy organisations

6

- Introduction
- Farewells
- Dismissals
- Giving a new colleague his place
- Breaking-up a team
- New teams
- Combining teams
- Splitting-up a business
- Change of culture
- Reorganisations
- The founder sells her business

6.1 Introduction

This is a book about exploring problems in organisations and how a consultant can contribute to revitalisation. Many of the systemic-phenomenological ideas and the techniques described are not only useful for solving problems but also for preventing them.

Primarily, this chapter is about the systemic approach as an instrument for leaders, administrators and managers. It is about everyday actions and interventions when everything in the garden is rosy and no consultant is involved.

Changes in organisations are the perfect moments to do justice to all that was, is and will be. When doing so you contribute to making a solid and vital system, that takes its place and is anchored in the outside world. In everyday life and work, many opportunities arise for minor interventions that bring about major systemic contributions. We discuss some frequently-occurring situations and offer suggestions for what a manager could do to strengthen the system, or to let it find a new balance. These are the kind of situations that can easily cause energy to leak out of the system when they do not receive sufficient attention.

6.2 Farewells

When someone has a place in an organisation and is going to leave that place, it is healthy, for the system and the person, to balance both sides of the transaction. By facing it as it is and then letting each other go:

- Sit in order of the most years of service to the least.

- Give the leaver the chance to say what he believes were his important contributions, what he was unable to do at his place and what he will take with him from his time in the organisation.

- The manager does the same. He also gives the leaver's colleagues the chance to say something personal about the leaver and also about the greater system of which they are a part.

- The leaver, in his current role, stands for a few moments behind his empty chair, then the manager puts this empty chair beside the last person to have joined the team or organisation: a new place awaiting a new colleague.

6.3 Dismissals

Fraud, sexual harassment, gross violation of the rules, deceit; these all happen and can be good reasons to dismiss someone, in some cases instantaneously. Certain behaviours are so unacceptable that there is no choice but to say *"You have to leave. Now."* Working from the systemic approach means paying attention to the fact the person did belong, that he had a place from where he contributed and that he did something that caused him to be dismissed.

- For xx years you belonged to our organisation and you contributed. Therefore we thank you.

- By what you did, you immediately forfeited your right to belong. That is why you have to leave now.

6.4 Giving a new colleague his place

Consider everywhere you have worked and how you were received in all those places. What helped you to settle in each new organisation? What didn't you have, or get, to be able to take your place fully?

Welcoming words could be:

- From now on this place is yours.

- This was someone else's place before you; we need a little time to adjust to the fact that it is now yours.

- This place has its own history. We'd love to tell you about it.

- You bring your own history and experience with you. We'd love to hear about it from you. You are welcome, with all your background. Now you belong with us. Thank you for your commitment!

6.5 Breaking-up a team

Usually it is senior management that decides whether a team continues or not. Perhaps there is no more budget or the goal has lost its importance, or the work can be done somewhere else better or cheaper and so on. In short, for the employees and the relevant part of the organisation it is over. Systems can easily bear many, far-reaching changes, if only everything, really everything, is faced. Then, usually, everyone and everything can go on, can continue.

- The person who makes the decision delivers the message.

- Connect the organisation's goals with what the employees and teams have contributed. Make it clear that this includes the pain, the burdens and the costs that the team carried.

- Express your thanks for everything the team and the employees invested, for what they always were contributing to the organisation.

- Nevertheless, taking everything into consideration, the time has come to stop. There are good reasons to do so. For this decision, the director/the management/the board accepts responsibility.

6.6 New teams

A new team has no history, it cannot have ... one might think. Isn't a new team oriented towards the future, full of new ambitions and new plans? However, looking back together provides a foundation from which to flow forward and to connect with the greater whole.

- Who decided to create the new team?

- Maybe there are people or departments who are paying a price for the creation of this team? Did another department lose? Were functions or budget taken from an existing department and given to the new team?

- How can everybody, who has contributed to the creation of the team, be recognised? Are people able to see and acknowledge those who offered resistance, who tried to stop it? Importantly, they provided the organisation with the test: do we really want/need this new team? Their resistance may have helped refine the structure and the tasks.

This way of recognising the new team connects it to the organisation and prevents it feeling better than the older teams, or better, even, than the organisation. A new team is often like an adolescent: inclined to overestimate himself; thinking he knows better than his parents and older siblings. Within an organisation, this can cause the system to indicate where the team should take its proper place, by opposing it. In this way, the system makes the new team aware that it needs the rest of the organisation. Giving recognition – at the start – can teach the team to take its proper place from the very beginning, full of competence and enthusiasm and, at the same time, embedded in the greater whole that also creates the framework.

6.7 Combining teams

Once there were two teams. Now they are one team. What is needed to weld two systems together into one? Often the approach is mainly forward-looking and focussed on identifying the connecting elements, on what is consistent. Systemically speaking, it is the history and the individual flavour of the old teams that give strength to the new team. Recognition for everything that already existed on both sides – like objectives, events, staff and clients – can help to combine the parts that will be useful and leave behind those that will not.

- Suggest each team presents itself to the other team: this is where we come from; this happened to us.

- Suggest each team tells or shows (maybe using symbols) what the members would love to bring into the new team and what they happily, or with regret, will leave behind.

- Suggest the 'listening' team recognises both the price the other team is paying and the value they are contributing.

6.8 Splitting-up a business

They have always belonged, yet now it seems logical for them to leave and find a different place. We find ourselves emphasising the logic of the new decision and trying to convince everyone of the benefits the split will produce. This feels 'right'; it shows that the issue of belonging is not being handled in a shallow way. Still, any split hurts. The closer the bond, the more painful the parting. You could see the pain as recognition of the bond. The more the pain is recognised, the more the old bond is acknowledged. Subsequently, it is helpful to make new commitments, new connections. How do we deal with the pain of parting and the pleasure of the new. First, by highlighting why it is right to split-up the company, then by acknowledging what the 'leaving' part has contributed to the whole:

- We see that you belonged.

- Because you belonged you were able to do all you did.

- There are good reasons to do it differently now.

- As an organisation we accept that we are losing your unique contribution. This causes pain.

- From now on, each part will walk its own path. I hope you, and us, can look back positively at the time that we were one.

6.9 Change of culture

A change process has a greater chance of success if it starts by acknowledging the old, especially when this is done by the initiators of the change:

- The present culture brought us to where we are now.

- The world has changed; we want and need to move with it.

- How we adapt is about how we treat each other and work together, the process where we will tread new paths. It asks all of us to let go of something we love.

- Change forces us to leave precious elements behind, causing us to mourn this loss. Let us stand together and, now and then, look back, instead of only pushing or pulling each other forward.

6.10 Reorganisations

What is a reorganisation? What can the initiator say about it?

- Existing connections will change or disappear.

- New connections have yet to take shape.

- The present order will change.

- New places will come into being; old places will disappear or will be embedded differently.

- The change from then to now is a sliding process of detaching, moving and re-anchoring.

- Originally, we started out with a clear connection to what we have on offer and what we have to do in the world surrounding us: we had lost touch with that connection; therefore this major transition is needed.

6.11 The founder sells her business

How difficult it is, when you are the owner, to let go of your business, your 'child' and to leave it to someone else! How easily you find yourself hanging-on to what you are trying to let go?

The founder handing over her business must take care to really let it go. Do not remain in a position of strategic adviser – not even for a short while. This is confusing for the new owner and the business in general. Say: *"I leave the company in your care. Do with it what you will."*

The new owner can help the founder to really let go. *"As the founder you made the company what it is now: very attractive to take over. You will always be the founder, without whom the business would not exist. I want to take it further, in my own way. Thank you for trusting me."*

Often, particularly in small firms, the employees have connected, heart and soul, to the owner/founder. How do you stop them feeling disloyal, when they must follow a direction that the founder would never have chosen?

In public, with the founder and the employees present, the new owner could say: *"Credit where credit is due: without the founder this business wouldn't have existed; without the workers it wouldn't have grown. Gladly, together with you and from this place, passed to me by the founder, I step into the future."*

Looking ahead

7

We are approaching the end of this book about systemic consulting.

Looking and thinking systemically has become a habit in the course of our professional development. Not only in our roles as consultants, coaches and trainers, but also in our everyday lives. We'd like to offer you some examples of how you could look systemically at the world around you.

7.1 Honoured or excluded?

In March 2011, the Dutch Education Ministry advised schools to give special recognition to those teachers who were head and shoulders above the rest. Every school had to identify its five per cent best teachers; they had to be teaching staff, not management or administration. They should be carefully chosen by their colleagues and management and the choices would be confirmed by an external review. Every school's annual top teacher would earn € 2,500 extra per year and, one day per week, he or she must inspire colleagues and help develop new teaching materials. This 'top teacher' would receive an annual budget of € 10,000 to spend on projects to improve teaching.

Awards create exclusion

What does it mean to the whole if a part, that was 'special' only in the sense that it performed its normal tasks very well, is encouraged to continue doing so by the award of extra salary?

How does this effect the contribution of the parts that are identified as not so good? Does the excellent teacher now belong more, or less, to the group of teachers? What happens if, in the following year, he or she is no longer judged as good enough to be in the group of excellent teachers? What is being recognised by this new policy and what is, perhaps, being ignored?

What becomes stronger? The school; the five per cent; the 95%; or the pupils? What is the price you pay for being judged as excellent ... or not excellent?

SIEBKE KAAT AND ANTON DE KROON

What happens to the quality of the whole, when ten per cent of the teachers in a school are 'excellent', but only five per cent are allowed to be called excellent? And what if nobody is head and shoulders above the rest? How would it feel if a young, recently-appointed teacher suddenly belonged to the 'excellent' group?

7.2 Everything where it belongs

All over the world, in museums, churches and private collections we find treasures that originally belonged to other countries, other cultures and other people. Often they are cherished and kept carefully. Sometimes they have been obtained via criminal action. What is clear, though, is that they belong somewhere else, whatever they might be: gold, silver, statues, books, the dead, archaeological objects, buildings or works of art.

How would it be if nations began a movement of returning and receiving?

Back home

The country giving back might say: "Through your ancestors, this belongs to you. Our ancestors misappropriated it.

It was precious to us and it was a pleasure to care for it. We now hand it back to you, to where it belongs."

The receiving country might say:

"Thank you for caring for it. We will handle it carefully, for our children. You are always welcome to come and see it again."

7.3 Without the old, the new wouldn't exist

The process of restructuring local government is often accompanied by much struggle and emotion. The energy put into the merging process is usually focussed on what the result should be, not on the price that will be paid.

Thank you

Would the process have a better chance of success if, first of all, attention was given to the origin and the individuality of all the separate parts that need to be brought together? How can their value be estimated and maintained? How can one build on that? How can the new organisation show its gratitude for all that each part contributes to the new local authority?

Once the reorganisation has become a fact, the new council usually works hard to shape its identity. The new name is promoted, the advantages named; every avenue of communication is used.

Where do we come from?

In the Netherlands, for example, there exists the newly-created municipality of Midden Drenthe. People living elsewhere in the country only have a vague idea where it is and of its boundaries. On their website it takes a lot of effort to find the list of villages and hamlets that make up the new municipality. Yet it is exactly these communities that have a connection with each other and with the rest of the country.

It is quite likely that a Dutch reader would recognise the names of villages like Westerbork (a World War II concentration camp) and Wijster (where a train was hijacked). But there are seventeen more villages that now belong to the new municipality. Plenty of Dutch people have, at some time in their lives, holidayed at one of these other villages and still feel a connection there. They know where the village is situated. But this connection is broken by bringing all these places together under the new name of Midden Drenthe. And we haven't even touched on the feelings of the inhabitants. They used to belong to their villages and that is how it still feels. What happens when that is 'ignored' as a result of the restructuring?

SIEBKE KAAT AND ANTON DE KROON

7.4 How do you choose where you want to belong?

A school recruits students with the slogan: *"Odulphus College builds your future."* Another school uses the text: *"King William I College; you will make it here."*

The hidden message

What place does the school take when it makes this statement? That it is working on the future of the student? (And not on something else, like developing his knowledge, but on the future, itself!?)

As a student at the King William I College, I must make it – but what if I'm not going to?

In both cases, what happens to the responsibilities of the students, the parents and the teachers?

7.5 Acknowledgement for the founder

Bart de Graaf, the founder of BNN, a young, modern Dutch broadcasting organisation, died in 2002. BNN honours him with a small museum in its head office. His special suits (due to a renal condition he was the size of a 12 year old) are on display, together with ornaments and photographs; 24/7, a TV in the museum shows the golden moments of his career. The day of his death continues to be commemorated: employees get the day off and BNN celebrates him by providing them with beer and snacks in a beach pub.

What do they celebrate?

The question here is: for how long does this ritual day-off strengthen the organisation? At what point does it just become an ordinary holiday for everyone, much like an average bank holiday? For how long can the

---

founder's original values, goals and wishes continue to be honoured, without always being connected to the person himself?

7.6 What to belong to; openly or anonymously?

In the Netherlands, citizens are intentionally invited – by reporting/informing about something they have seen or know – to belong to something to which they might not openly choose to belong. Report Crimes Anonymously is an independent hotline that passes information to the police. Callers can report people they know personally and can do so anonymously.

Example

Choosing where you want to belong seems to be an exciting story.

Reporting anonymously sounds like running with the hare and hunting with the hounds: not damaging the relationship with another person (perhaps because the price would be too high), but also not putting the relationship with society on the line by remaining silent. How is it to belong to two systems that don't want to belong together? What is the cost of informing?

How widely has education adopted the idea that children should learn not to be telltales? How many children try to get into the good books of their parents or friends (increase their belonging to them) just by telling tales? What kind of parent is able to totally disregard information received this way? What happens if a parent fishes for this kind of information from a child?

7.7 What place do you get? What place do you take?

Dutch local authorities are often referred to as lower government. This implies, of course, a higher government. Lately, local authorities have started referring to themselves as first government.

Which place do you give someone else by choosing your own name?

SIEBKE KAAT AND ANTON DE KROON

7.8 In balance?

A captain of industry is, usually, not the available husband and father his family might want. In such a case it is likely that the husband and wife will look for a good way to be there for each other and their family. In one such situation, the wife committed herself to care for the family completely alone. It gave her husband the opportunity to be completely available for the company. He, in turn, tried to balance the situation by saying to his wife: *"You can write my resignation letter now and I'll keep it on my desk."* His idea was that he would submit the letter when his wife said she could no longer cope.

A solution for what?

Did the wife's place become lighter? Would the husband give more, or less consideration to the effect his work had on his partner's life?

7.9 The framework within which everything functions

Q-fever is a disease primarily affecting goats; a small number of people also have died from it. When an action plan, for possible future outbreaks, was being prepared, there was fierce infighting to decide which ministry should take the lead: the Ministry of Agriculture or the Ministry of Health.

The first place is more important than the second place. The first creates the framework within which the second must function.

7.10 Who is there for whom?

A beautiful and atmospheric 19th century building in a big city. Scores of volunteers are unselfishly involved in putting the building to good use as a centre for conferences, training courses and meetings. Each and everyone sees themselves as being a part of the alternative culture. For quite some time the building has been doing well financially.

However, a growing number of the building's paying customers are becoming increasingly unhappy. They get the feeling that they are there for the volunteers, instead of the volunteers being there to serve them, the paying customers.

Giving and taking in a fair balance?

Is it possible to engage in something, unselfishly, for a long time? Can the systemic need for balance endure only giving, when the taking is looking for a way out?

7.11 A pattern?

A boy comes home from school with a note for his parents: *"Your son is dyslexic and this is the year of his final exams. You are welcome to discuss this issue with his mentor, the day after tomorrow, from 10.15 till 10.45 a.m. The date and time cannot be changed."*

The note is signed by the mentor; it contains no telephone number or e-mail address.

What is their place?

What is the place of parents at secondary schools? Do they belong? If so, in what places? Teachers, a little tentatively, speak about two types of parents: those that push their children too much and demand a lot of the teacher's attention, and those that fail in their parenting and leave it to the school to solve their problems. Is this, perhaps, a symptom that shows there is no clear place for the parents, rather than that parents want or don't want to be involved?

Does the struggle to give each other a place mirror the pupil's puberty process, which he undergoes during this period, where he will be looking at what place to give his parents in his life?

SIEBKE KAAT AND ANTON DE KROON

Is a pattern repeating here? Perhaps the parents, the teacher and the pupil, all of them, feel that they are constantly failing?

7.12 Belonging to those that do not belong

UNPO (Unrepresented Nations and Peoples Organisation) represents the interests of countries and nations that are not affiliated with any international organisation. Not because they don't want to be, but because they are not recognised, by the greater whole, for what they are. Zanzibar, Estonia and Eastern Timor are countries that have recently received such recognition. There are some fifty peoples and countries that, as far as a large part of the rest of the world is concerned, do not belong. The Moluccan Islands and Tibet are well-known examples.

All of us belong

All over the world people have different views about what belongs and what does not belong. A lot of blood has been spilled around claiming and being granted a place. The process leaves open wounds and the ensuing traumas leave deep scars.

How would it be, wherever one lives in the world, to say to each other:

"Yes, we all belong to this earth and this entitles us to a place. Just like you, we really want to keep our individuality and to connect with the greater whole. We want to find out how to create a healthy balance between being together and being separate, between mutual exchange and the preservation of that which determines our identity."

7.13 Acknowledging everything

Phyllis Rodriguez, an American mother, lost her son in the 9-11 attack on the World Trade Center. Soon afterwards, she started to worry about what her country might do in her son's name.

Zacarias Moussaoui, regarded to be 'the 20th hijacker' – was in the plane they intended to crash into the White House. His mother, Aisha el-Wafi, came to the United States when she learned that the American government would insist on the death penalty for her son if he was found guilty.

Phyllis and her husband spoke out against the death penalty for Moussaoui and felt admiration for the woman who dared to enter this hostile country to stand by her son.

Later both mothers met. Each one said to the other: *"As a mother you have suffered a great deal."*

Based on an article in the Trouw newspaper, 13th of August 2011.

Yes

Acknowledgement of all that is; by both sides.

No claim of a bigger grief.

There is enough to do without settling scores.

Appendixes

A

A.1 About the authors

Anton about Siebke

Siebke's approach to systemic-phenomenological work is very pure. Being straight and pure in a doctrine does not always manifest in a positive way. Often it comes with a dogmatic attitude and messages that are attuned more to the doctrine than the people for whom they are meant.

But, with Siebke it is a very different experience: she radiates complete acceptance and space for whatever there is. Her extremely sensitive systemic radar permanently scans everything, searching for patterns and points of systemic recognition. She does this while connected and, simultaneously, while keeping a distance.

As a trainer she moves effortlessly between theory and practice. All without judgement and with all the other, very necessary, qualities about which you have read in this book. She truly is a leading person in the world of systemic work. Any client would be delighted to have her as their consultant.

Collaborating on this book was a supple process. We took our time to discuss everything fundamentally, to formulate and reformulate. Major parts of the book were completely rewritten, often several times. This made it better, sharper and more precise. And through this process it really became our book. Of course I recognise my own examples and phrases, but the whole is the result of a beautiful process of co-creation. This book is not the only result; my professional skills have grown as well.

I am happy that Siebke took the first step towards the book. I would never have started it on my own.

Some facts. What is her work history? Where does she belong?

Siebke was born in 1961. She graduated in social psychology from the Free University of Amsterdam. From 1987 onwards she has worked in and for several large organisations as a trainer, (team) coach and consultant. At the Institute for Communications at Kortrijk (Belgium) she followed the advanced training course Management of Groups, based on systemic theory, and the basic training in Gestalt therapy.

After some years she gave up her position as a trainer and consultant to become Director of the University for Natural Medicine in Arnhem. In 2001, together with some colleagues, she set up her own business, Pragmavision. She specialises in themes like workplace harassment, support after traumatic experiences at work and coaching teams and individuals to regain their own strength. She participated in the Dutch Bert Hellinger Institute's year-long training, System Dynamics in Organisations, after which she participated in several advanced training courses in facilitating constellations. Since 2010 she has been, together with Anton de Kroon, a trainer at the Dutch Bert Hellinger Institute. She is married with two sons.

Siebke about Anton

Anton is a mild person. Everything people do or don't do he truly does see as arising out of love and loyalty, even when their actual behaviour is unacceptable. His attitude is neither fake nor a role. He takes everyone into his heart; you can feel this. Anton is the basic systemic attitude.

Anton is also very careful and precise. Before he speaks, he lets a sentence filter through him and tests it to see if it has the right taste ... do these words really say what we want them to? Could someone reading it give it a different accent, a different meaning? So, working, thinking and writing together, our images, thoughts and experiences became words and, in turn, the words were filled with thoughts, images and experiences, through which new insights appeared.

Anton is familiar with organisational systems from within and without. He knows about the struggles of management, the special position of the interim manager, the possibilities and difficulties of really cooperating in a team, the pleasant and difficult position of a consultant or a coach. The concept of everyone in his own place, as the basis of a powerful system, is an insight born out of his real life.

Anton also is a man of much life-experience. What is ... is. He has the courage to face up to whatever is there, in himself and in others. And then, all of a sudden, there are new possibilities either to continue or to say farewell. Movements arising from the courage to look reality directly in the eyes.

Without Anton this book would not be in existence. He was the engine of progress.

Some facts. Where does he come from?

Anton de Kroon was born in 1943. At the turn of the century he began to make himself familiar with systemic work via various training courses. Since 2007 he has been closely involved with the Dutch Bert Hellinger Institute, leading training courses and workshops both at home and abroad and, since 2010, regularly with Siebke Kaat.

For fourteen years he was a partner in Greep Management and Organisational Development, bringing with him his own practice and his own special skills. As a consultant and coach he worked substantially in first and second-line health care organisations.

His professional roots are in psychology and sociology. From the very beginning, his professional life has been one of continuous development and learning. The results of this approach are visible in his career as professional worker, coordinator, team leader, manager (with ever-growing responsibilities), consultant, trainer and mentor.

About the (systemic) editor: James Campbell

Language is a wonder. Although we all might speak the same mother tongue, we do so each in our own unique way. Face to face, we have many tools to ensure we understand and are understood. But reading another's text presents us with the challenge of understanding the author's intentions rather than giving his or her words our own meaning, without those checks and balances. This is where the role of the editor comes in and it is a responsibility and challenge I enjoy. I see my job as doing as little as possible to a text while ensuring that the author's meaning comes through to as many readers as possible, whether they are reading in English as their mother tongue or their second, or even third, language.

I'm constantly checking with myself (and, when necessary, with the author) that my opinions, beliefs and ideas are not slipping into the book unnoticed. At the same time I try to make the book easier to read by giving it flow and removing ambiguities. English versions of books tend to be the ones upon which further translations are based and this, too, informs and conditions how I edit. In the way that I work (I can't speak for other editors) there comes a point in the editing process when everything comes together in a kind of gestalt: the book emerges out of the letters,

spaces, words and sentences, I can enjoy and appreciate it as a whole...
and I know, then, we are almost home.

I was born in London in 1950 of Scottish parents and now live in an intentional community, in Eindhoven, the Netherlands, with my wife and 6-year-old daughter. I grew up playing football, mountain-biking and reading poetry. Football is now limited to watching Manchester United, the Netherlands has no mountains, but the joy, inspiration and support I find in poetry increases with each passing year.

I first experienced systemic work, in the form of constellations, around 1998, and in the ensuing 15 years or so I have followed many training courses and workshops, especially with Judith Hemming and Jan Jacob Stam. I've been working as a general (English Language) editor for about 10 years. My earlier activities include studying for a BSc in Chinese Medicine and many years of global sales management roles. My life always feels lighter in those moments when I feel here and true contact can occur. James can be contacted at `james@jamesgcampbell.eu`

A.2 Our sources of inspiration

- Boszormenyi-Nagy, Ivan; Krasner, Barbara,
  Between give and take. A clinical guide to contextual therapy,
  New York (Brunner/Mazel) 1986

- Brenters, Marlies,
  De organisatie als netwerk. Hoe mensen organisaties veranderen en organisaties mensen,
  Alphen aan den Rijn (Samsom) 1999

- Bryan, Bill; Goodman, Michael; Schaveling, Jaap,
  Systeemdenken. Ontdekken van onze organisatiepatronen,
  Den Haag (Academic Service) 2009

- Capra, Fritjof,
  The Web of Life: A New Scientific Understanding of Living Systems,
  New York (Achor Books) 1996

- Choy Joep (red.),
  De vraag op het antwoord. Systemische interventies voor conflicten in organisaties,
  Santpoort Zuid (NISTO) 2005

- Chungliang Al Huang; Lynch, Jerry,
  Mentoring, the tao of giving and receiving wisdom,
  New York (Harper Collins Publishers) 1995

- Franke, Ursula,
  The River Never Looks Back. Historical and Practical Foundations of Bert Hellinger's Family Constellations,
  Heidelberg (Carl-Auer Verlag) 2009

- Hellinger, Bert,
  Die Quelle braucht nicht nach dem Weg zu fragen,
  Heidelberg (Carl-Auer Verlag) 2001

- Hellinger, Bert; Weber, Gunthard; Franke-Griksch, Marianne; Mahr, Albrecht; Schneider, Jakob,
  Leven zoals het is. Werken met familieopstellingen, organisatieopstellingen en consultatieopstellingen,
  Groningen (Het Noorderlicht) 2002

- Hellinger, Bert,
  Mitte und mass,
  Heidelberg (Carl-Auer Verlag) 1999

- Hellinger, Bert,
  De kunst van het helpen,
  Groningen (Het Noorderlicht) 2004

- Hellinger, Bert,
  Der grosse Konflikt, die Antwort,
  München (Goldman Verlag) 2005

- Hellinger, Bert,
  Hellinger Sciencia,
  Heidelberg (Carl-Auer-Systeme)

- Hellinger, Bert,
  Erfolge im Leben / Beruf,
  Bisschofswiesen (Hellinger Publications)

- Holitzka, Marlies en Remmert, Elisabeth,
  Systemische organisatieopstellingen. Conflicten oplossen in en op het werk,
  Katwijk (Panta Rhei) 2004

- Homan, Thijs,
  Organisatiedynamica. Theorie en praktijk van organisatieverandering,
  Den Haag (Academic Service) 2008

- Jaworski, Joseph,
  Synchronicity. The Inner Path of Leadership,
  San Francisco (Berrett-Koehler publishers) 1998

- Kampen, Joost,
  Verwaarloosde organisaties. Introductie van een nieuw concept voor organisatieprofessionals,
  Deventer (Kluwer) 2011

- Minuchin, Salvador & H. Charles Fishman,
  Families and Family Therapy, a Strtuctural Approach,
  1973

- Morgan, Gareth,
  Images of Organization,
  (SAGE Publication Inc.) 1986

- Morris, Desmond,
  The Human Zoo,
  1994

- Perls, Fritz,
  Gestalt Therapie Verbatim,
  Lafayette Calif. (Real People Press) 1969.

- Rosselet, Claude; Senoner, Georg,
  Enacting Solutions. Management Constellations, an innovative approach to problem-solving and decision-making in organizations,
  (Edizioni Ledizioni Ledi Publishing) 2013

- Satir, Virginia,
  People Making,
  Palo Alto (Science and Behavior Books Inc.) 1972

- Scharmer, C. Otto,
  Theory U. Learning from the Future as it Emerges,
  Cambridge, Massachusetts (SOL) 2007

- Schaveling, Jaap,
  Tijdelijk leiderschap. Dienstbaarheid aan mens en organisatie,
  Den Haag (SDU Uitgevers b.v.) 2008

- Seattle,
  The Speech of Chief Seattle,
  (Applewood Books) 2003

- Senge, Peter; Scharmer, C. Otto; Jaworski, Joseph; Flowers, Betty Sue,
  Presence. Exploring profound change in people, organizations and society,
  Cambridge, Massachusetts (SOL) 2004

- Sparrer, Insa; Varga von Kibéd, Matthias,
  Klare Sicht in Blindflug. Schriften zur Systemische Strukturaufstellung,
  Heidelberg (Carl-Auer Verlag) 2010

- Stam, Jan Jacob,
  Fields of Connection. The practice of organisational Constellations,
  Groningen (het Noorderlicht) 2006

- Stam, Jan Jacob,
  Vleugels voor verandering. Organisatieontwikkeling vanuit een Systemisch Perspectief,
  Groningen (het Noorderlicht) 2012

- Varga von Kibéd, Matthias; Sparrer, Insa, Ganz im Gegenteil,
  Tetralemmaarbeit und andere Grundformen Systemischer Strukturaufstellungen – für Querdenker und solche, die es werden wollen,
  Heidelberg (Carl-Auer Verlag) 2005

- Weber, Gunthard,
  Praxis der Organisationsaufstellungen,
  Heidelberg (Carl-Auer-Systeme Verlag) 2000

- Weick, Karl,
  The social psychology of organizing,
  Reading (Addison-Wesley) 1979

- Whittington, John,
  Systemic Coaching & Constellations. An introduction to the principles, practices and application,
  London (Kogan Page) 2012

A.3 About the Dutch Bert Hellinger Institute

The Bert Hellinger Institute the Netherlands (BHIN) was founded by Jan Jacob Stam and Bibi Schreuder in 2000 and since 2015, Barbara Hoogenboom is co-owner.

Bert Hellinger encouraged Jan Jacob to take this step and allowed him to use his name. To this day, we are in regular contact and exchange with Bert Hellinger, now 91 years old.

What characterizes BHIN is:

- On the one hand, the loyalty to the foundation of the systemic phenomenological work the way Bert Hellinger discovered and described it. Working with the consciences, the principles (workings) and the patterns that arise;

- On the other hand, the continuing, phenomenological, openness to what wants to develop and reveal itself. This means for example, that we look at this work and the role of facilitator in constellations in a different way than in 2000. And that we have said our farewell to habits and interventions that were previously customary.

We can imagine, and even encourage the participants in our courses, to incorporate systemic work in their 'own toolkit' with their other 'tools'. That they develop their own style and mix. But with the implicit assumption that people are clear in their communication about their mixture.

This is only possible, if at BHIN we stay, as purely and precisely as possible, close to the foundations or the phenomenological work. That is what we enjoy most, and with a lot of love. Ánd that is what we want people to recognise us for, both meanings of the word, in the outside world.

More information and contact:
info@hellingerinstituut.nl
www.hellingerinstituut.nl

A.4 About Systemic Books

Systemic Books is an international independent Publishing House focused on creating high quality content selected from the broad range of books available. The books range from classic to cutting edge work with new adaptations of the systemic school of thought and working. This way, Systemic Books aims to answer to the different levels of knowledge people have or need on systemic work.

Systemic Books wass founded in joint energy by Siets Bakker and Barbara Piper in 2016. When they met in 2015, their knowledge of and interest in the systemic perspective and their shared love for books, planted the seed for Systemic Books. This initiative combines their knowledge in the publishing world and efforts to make systemic work available to a global audience. We translate, edit and publish books. Great books about the systemic school of thought. We make use of all modern possibilities in publishing and printing to make these books available all over the world.

More information and contact:
`contact@systemicbooks.com`
`www.systemicbooks.com`

Printed in Great Britain
by Amazon